Alister & Lisa,

Hope you are both

enjoy the read

Jonathan

REMEMBER HOW IT GOES?

Jonathan Frazer

Remember How It Goes?

UNDERSTANDING THE BIBLE ANEW

the columba press

First published in 2015 by
the columba press
55A Spruce Avenue,
Stillorgan Industrial Park,
Blackrock, Co. Dublin

Cover by David Mc Namara
Origination by The Columba Press
Printed by scandBook AB, Sweden

ISBN 978 1 78218 233 7

*To my wife Naomi,
for your encouragement, support, wisdom and love.*

Prologue

This didn't start off being a book.

It started off with me reading through the Bible in a year.

It was something I'd always wanted to do and as I read it, I discovered that there really is a story behind it all, and it was a story I wanted to share.

It's a story full of hope.

Of joy.

Of promises.

But it's also a story that's filled with sadness.

And tears.

And frustrations.

And questions.

Whenever I talk to people about the Bible, or, because of my job, when people talk to me about the Bible, they often focus on how out of touch and out of date it is and God is. It's just an old book, written long ago, about some people in a far off land, dealing with a God who isn't here, or isn't interested anymore!

What we often don't realise is that in the midst of it all are some shocking similarities with the world that we know and inhabit.

When we look at the world around us it doesn't take us long before we see things that catch our attention.

Things that make us ask 'What's going on?'

We can tell that things aren't right.

We can tell that things aren't the way they're supposed to be.

And when we look at our own lives we are often faced with the same questions:

Why did we lose our job?

Our house?

Our loved one?

Why did things not go the way I wanted?

Often we ask these questions into the vacuum and to no one in particular, but often they have an edge, an anger, because we aim them at someone.

And usually that person's name is

God.

Why did He let this happen?

Why didn't He step in?

Is He good at all?

Is He here at all?

When we read the Bible, the book that tells us about Him and His ways, we discover that we are not the only ones who have asked these questions; in fact there is story after story of people who for thousands of years have gone through exactly what we have, and asked exactly the same questions that we have.

That is the shocking part!

We discover

We are not alone.

It's maybe not so different and random as we thought.

This thing, which has ended up taking the form of a book, takes us through some of those stories in the hope that through them we see and realise that God has not given up on this place.

On this creation of His.

On these people.

On us.

My hope is that as we read through these stories we discover that God is still creating something new and is drawing us to be part of it.

To be part of a whole new world.

Contents

Let Me Introduce Eddie

CHAPTER ONE

There is an advert on TV which I occasionally see about the National Lottery. I'm sure many of you have seen it where there is a man called Eddie whose face is all you can see. We are told that Eddie didn't go out the week that his lottery numbers came up but as the camera pans out we see that Eddie is in fact lying on a masseur's table being massaged by two ladies all while lying on a yacht anchored in crystal blue waters off a beautiful island.

Eddie played online.

Eddie won a lot of money.

And the way Eddie spent it was to buy a yacht, have several ladies to massage him on his command and the chances are he's bought the island as well.

Eddie seems like a pretty normal guy.

But his life has been transformed by this win.

Eddie is living the dream.

Good job he played online.

We say this because Eddie looks pretty normal and we have the idea that Eddie worked a fairly typical nine-to-five job, which he probably didn't enjoy much, he maybe had to work weekends to support a family and, although he looks like he eats pretty well, he usually spends his Friday and Saturday nights in the local pub trying to forget about the week he's had and enjoy the moments as they come. He ends up watching a lot of TV and stays up late to watch the programmes he wants after everyone else goes to bed. He even struggles out of bed on those cold winter months when he has to go out early to defrost the cars while everyone else turns over in the heat of their beds.

We say this about Eddie because at times this is how we feel.

We project our story onto his.

And so when Eddie gets the chance, presumably having played the lottery for many years previous, and gets the call or email to say he's won this fortune he either doesn't speak for a few minutes from shock or he shouts for all he's got because now he will be able to live the dream.

But what is the dream?

For Eddie the dream obviously revolves around this yacht sitting in crystal blue waters off a beautiful island while the sun beats down on his well-massaged back. The wife and the kids I'm guessing are below deck or they are in the water in the speedboat doing a bit of wakeboarding, allowing him a little quiet time with the masseurs.

This is his dream.

But remember that we project our story onto his.

So the chances are this is our dream too.

The yacht.

The island.

The crystal blue waters.

And the two masseurs of specific genders.

This is what we dream of, not because we specifically like lying on a yacht or indeed owning islands but because this gets us out of the worlds that we inhabit every single day.

Eddie has been able to get away from the drudgery of his life and so we dream of being able to do the same.

We project our story onto his.

It doesn't matter which island we anchor off, it doesn't even matter the size of the yacht as long as we can escape to somewhere better.

Escape.

Because our lives aren't interesting, they are consumed with work and deadlines, with pressure from our bosses to hit targets and make more than we do already. Pressure from our spouses to do more than we do when we get home. Pressure from our children to spend more time with them. Pressure to look after our children because their father walked out with another woman. Pressure to cope after the loss of someone we thought we never could live without. Pressure to keep up with what everyone else has. The world we live in tells us that we need all these things to be happy.

We need a good job.

We need to be a perfect wife.

To have perfect children.

To have looks.

The chiselled body.

Money.

And more money.

And when we can't get these things, or when we can't get enough of them and when they let us down we can't cope because we don't think we're good enough, or we've let people down, or we've failed; the only option left is to escape.

Escape.

And it doesn't even have to be because of these reasons, it may be something much more simple than that.

Jealousy.

Tiredness.

Loneliness.

There can be any number of reasons but we feel that, if we can escape, things can be different, so we spend our precious spare time looking through holiday magazines, looking for somewhere perfect to get away so we can recharge or get some headspace for a few days. To be able to go somewhere where there is no pressure to hit targets or even cook for our families. Our troubles will not find us when we're snorkelling in the tropical blue seas, and the only panic will be when to put on the next layer of suntan lotion.

It all seems idyllic as we leaf through the pages, as we plan the trip, as we pack our bags and head to the airport, but when the holiday comes to an end, we feel the weight slowly creeping into our bodies and minds, because when we return home things will be no different to when we left.

It happens in a miniature form on a Sunday night as well, the Sunday night blues that we get when we realise that the weekend is over and the harsh reality is that we go back to work tomorrow and the never-ending cycle will start up again.

We can never really escape.

Unless!

We play the lottery.

Because look at Eddie.

Look how things turned out for him.

Things turned out pretty sweet for him.

He's living the dream.

He's happy.

So we pick our numbers and pay our pounds hoping that we too will be able to cash it all in and one day be like Eddie who's holiday will never end, who doesn't have to face 'real life' anymore.

How did it all end up like this?

Because it's fiction.

Or is it?

Can we simply say its good advertising, or does this really happen?

Maybe we have to talk about a home-grown hero.

George Best was a cult hero in Northern Ireland, and still is despite his premature death in 2005, but there's an infamous story about him that has taken on almost myth-like status, even though he told it himself on many occasions.

It goes like this.

George was on a well-earned break in Vegas with his lady of the time, who happened to be Miss World.

As you do.

After a successful night on the tables they both retired to the hotel room and George ordered a bottle of champagne to help celebrate his winnings. When the porter, who was also from Northern Ireland, appeared at the door with the champagne he was greeted by George, thousands of pounds worth of notes strewn across the bed and a scantily clad Miss World. He poured the champagne and after receiving a healthy tip from George went to leave the room, but as he got to the door he stopped, turned shaking his head and said:

'Where did it all go wrong Georgie, where did it all go wrong?'

That is not what we might say

We would ask, 'Where did it all go right George?'

'What numbers did you play to end up with all this?'

For it seemed George was also living the dream. He probably had the yacht to go back to and had no real troubles in life, or so it seemed at that time.

It wasn't fiction for Georgie and the many others like him.

Is this what we dream about?

Is this what we long for?

Is this what we see as the pinnacle of life?

How did it end up like this for them?

How did it end up like this for us?

Hold that thought.

In the first book of the Bible the whole story is introduced with a detailed account of a world, this world that God creates. Whether you read it as a story or poem or some kind of anti-story does not really matter, the important thing to see and to keep as the central aspect of it all is that this God creates not because he has to, not because his arm is twisted and he has no other choice, but because he wants to.

On the first 'day' God creates light and separates the light from the darkness, calling the light 'day' and the darkness 'night'.

And He calls it 'good'.

On the second day He creates an expanse that separates the water from water and He calls this expanse 'sky'.

And He calls it 'good'.

On the third day He gathers the waters together until dry land appears and makes this land produce vegetation, plants and fruit trees.

And He calls it 'good'.

On the fourth He creates.

On the fifth day He creates.

On the sixth day He creates.

And He calls it all 'good'.

On the seventh day God sits back and looks over all that He has done, like a master painter or artist who has finished the work after a long time of putting it all together, of forming it, of refining it, of touching up the little bits, He sits back and says that it's all 'good'.

What we have here is an account of what happened, no one saw it first-hand, apart from God Himself, and reported to all their friends what happened, but what we have is an account of what took place. Of course, because it is an account, there are many theories surrounding it and what it might mean. One of my favourites is the *Enuma Elish*, where the true meaning lies in a story where the earth is formed from the corpse of a murdered god. The details aren't important, but it goes to show that there are more narratives about creation than just the Christian narrative. So we must look at this Christian narrative of creation in light of when and why it was written, but here, as I mentioned before we look to the central aspect of God as creator who calls His creation 'good'.

In the original language the word 'good' is the word *tob*.

Whenever we translate any word from any language into English, and vice versa, we lose some of its meaning, some of its fullness. Any word that we translate carries with it understanding and years of use in various context and understanding.

Take the word 'love' for example which we have in English. When we, as native speakers of English use this word we have a wide variety of contexts in which we use it. We say that we love our spouse, our parents, our children, but equally we say that we love ice cream, we love leaves on an autumn day, we love lamp.[1]

When someone who is not a native speaker goes to translate this word they will be totally confused as to how to do it, unless they understand the context and the way it is being used. If they don't do this, they may think we love leaves in the same way we love our children.

So when we translate this word, *tob*, we need to be wary of simply saying it means good, because it means more than that.

It means completeness or perfection.

When it is used in this sense in this creation story it means that God looked at what He had created and saw that it was complete.

Exactly as He wanted it.

Perfect.

Not in an 'it's near enough' kind of way, or 'it's good, but not perfect' way. God looked at His finished work and knew it was perfect, there were no flaws, there were no bits that had to be remoulded or redone and so because of that knowledge, because of that word, *tob*, God could rest, satisfied in the knowledge that everything was perfect.

Did I leave anything out?

Well maybe I left *someone* out.

His name was Adam.

In this story of creation, Adam was the pinnacle of God's creative energy, he was the pinnacle of this *tob*, and he was made in the image of God himself,[2] given attributes that were unlike anything else within this creation and having the breath of life breathed into his nostrils.[3] He was put in charge of the fish of the sea and the birds of the air and over the livestock and every creeping thing on earth.[4]

He was a pretty important part of creation.

He was also given a pretty important role in creation and that was to tend this garden that he found himself in, the Garden of Eden. Even at the very start of creation and as part of God's plan there was work which Adam had to do and with it all there was one condition:

Do not eat from the fruit of one tree.[5]

Seems pretty manageable doesn't it?

If that seems easy and the work seems hard, he even got a helper, a woman called Eve.[6]

They had a beautiful relationship with each other and with God and it seems to be that they had such an intimate relationship with God that they were able to walk in the cool of the day with Him.

This creation, this garden, was *tob*.

Perfect.

That was, until a serpent enters the story.

This serpent questions the one condition that was put on them about this one tree. He seems pretty convincing and tells Eve that it's all a bunch of lies, there is no truth in it at all and you won't actually die, what will really happen is that you'll become like God, able to know good and evil. From this point, it's easy to see the slippery slope and it's easy to see how the ego has been massaged.

Eve wants to become like God.

And so when she sees that the tree is good for fruit and was a delight to her eyes, she takes and eats the fruit and shares it with Adam.

What a nice gesture!

Before this happened, creation was *tob*.

From here on in the story, this creation is no longer *tob*.

It has been broken.

We are told that once their eyes had been opened they realise their nakedness and make themselves clothes, even hiding from God as they hear Him walking in the garden.

This is a point when we see the remarkable humility of God.

As He walks in the garden, He calls out for Adam and Eve to see where they are. We would imagine He already knows but He asks the question anyway.

Adam and Eve's response shows what they have done as God hears how they have taken fruit from the tree, eaten and have gained knowledge, realising that they were naked and hiding from Him.

This one condition seemed too hard to keep and as a result they are expelled from the garden.

This perfect creation that God had created has been broken and ruined.

We live in the result of that decision.

The world in which we find ourselves is a result of that choice.

That is why we have an uneasy feeling.

That is why we have dissatisfaction.

That is why we have a longing for that sense of *tob*.

It all comes from that choice.

When we see that advert with Eddie and we long for something perfect, it is not the beach or the yacht or the masseurs that we long for; it is the longing for that uneasy feeling to disappear.

What was once a perfect world has now become broken, messed up, chaotic.

In recent days, as I have been writing this there have been many things that have been happening in the world that are hard to get our human minds around.

Twenty children between the ages of six and seven were gunned down while in their classrooms along with six teachers.

A 29-year-old died from skin cancer after battling it for over four years.

Protestors in Belfast have been throwing petrol bombs, stones, fireworks and whatever else they can get their hands on, at police and onlookers. Of those who were protesting, many of them were children.

These are only a few stories that I have been aware of in the last few days and throughout the world that we live in, I'm sure we could recount and tell many other stories. We watch the news, local and national, and see nothing but violence and war, of people who wage hatred against each other, and that's only the news that the media want us to see, that only covers a fraction of what goes on in the world:

There's hunger.

Famine.

Lack of water.

Lack of basic hygiene.

Lack of clothing.

There are statistics that say things aren't the way they should be:

783 million people in the world do not have access to clean water, that's a tenth of the world's population.

2.5 billion people in the world do not have access to adequate sanitation, that's two fifths of the world's population.[7]

The statistics go on.

And on.

And on.

Things are not the way they should be.

At these times we ask:

'Where is God in all of this?'

'What is He doing?'

'Why did He let this happen?'

As we ask these questions we know that all is not *tob*, all is not perfect. In fact, things are far from perfect, so what is going on?

It is these questions that we seek and that will ring in our ears as we travel together through the Bible to see what God is doing, if anything at all, in this world. I will tell you now that there are other books and publications that put forward arguments and philosophical debates to answer these questions and so if that is what you are looking for I can direct you to those, but what we seek to do is to walk through the Bible to see how these questions play out, because the Bible tells us something about the world. It isn't a very old book that tells us a little bit of history; but it's a book that tells us about God and about how God interacts with the world.

God created the world.

It is His.

But things are not the way He wants them to be.

Sorry?

CHAPTER TWO

I was walking in the centre of Belfast a number of years ago and in front of the City Hall is a large grassy area which leads out onto the main street. In it they often put on shows and in the winter months leading up to Christmas there's a continental market which comes and trades in it as well. This grassy area also allows for protests but that's not something that's encouraged!

As I was walking past on this occasion I happened to notice that there was some kind of art exhibition on and so dandered through to see what there was, and there I was met with the most amazing and fascinating piece of art.

I am not a connoisseur of art and wouldn't claim to be anything of an artist, that's a gene that bypassed me and went to my sisters, but I do like art, the more random the better.

Sat on this grassy area was a large ball held by two hands, but it wasn't as boring as that sounds; the ball, which must've been at least four metres in diameter, was made of old computer screens and printers, keyboards and hoovers and microwaves and many other electrical appliances. The hands holding this ball were made of metal but were covered in electronic chipboards and leads.

For some reason I was fascinated by this.

All these things had been discarded and thrown away by someone, treated as being too old to be of use, or they were broken and not worth fixing; yet there was another person who had collected them and bought them, stored them up, shaped them and seen value in them and made them come alive again.

To me, it was an amazing creation.

To me it tells us something about God.

When Adam and Eve sinned, when they had taken this fruit from the tree and eaten it, wanting to become like God, they had taken the *tob* from creation and made it broken, destroying everything about it that had been made good. For that reason they had been expelled from the garden.

The creation that He had made was no longer *tob*.

It was broken.

When they did that, God could have started again.

No one could blame Him, and no one would say anything to Him about trying again, starting over again for a second time. Like those people who threw away their electrical appliances, they didn't have any second thoughts, they only knew that something better could be bought and so they don't think twice about discarding their old appliance; in fact it's probably cheaper and easier to buy something new than to get it repaired anyway!

In this society that we live in today, everything is discarded and thrown away with such ease that we couldn't say a word to God about wanting to discard this creation, but what He saw in it was something more than that, something worth saving. Like the artist who collected and bought and stored all those appliances to make that piece of art, God, who is a master creator, saw beauty in the midst of this broken creation; He saw life in the midst of decay, and for the value that He saw in it, He did not give up and start again.

What we see in the rest of the Bible comes from that insight about God. Everything that comes after, comes about because God doesn't want to give up on what He had created. He doesn't want to throw it away and discard it like a broken computer, but He wants to make it right, to renew it and see it *tob* once again.

We even see this play out in the very next sentences in Genesis.

When Adam and Eve were expelled from the garden we are told that they weren't even destroyed for their disobedience but they get to go on with their lives. God could have started again with new humans, people who would listen and pay attention to God's warnings, but He didn't. He expelled them instead.

So they go about their lives.

Adam and Eve did what married couples sometimes do as they go about their lives and they had a son and named him Cain.

Then Eve had another son and named him Abel.

It's interesting that the first thing we are told about these two boys is that Cain is a worker of the ground and Abel is a worker of the sheep. These were the things their parents were supposed to be doing in the garden and so here we can see that the two boys are taking over what the parents have done, but in the hope that they can do it better.

We can see that God didn't want to give up on them because the first thing we see them do, once we've found out what their job is, is bring an offering to God; Cain brought some of the fruit from the ground and Abel brought the firstborn of his flock and some of their fat portions.

At surface level there doesn't seem to be much wrong, there doesn't seem to be much difference between the two but we are told God 'had regard for Abel and his offering, but for Cain and his offering he had no regard'.[8]

It seems strange that God would do that.

It seems He favours one and not the other; they both bring an offering, so why does He choose one over the other?

The answer lies in how they bring their offering.

Abel brings the firstborn from his flock, the very first thing that came from the flock and sets it apart to God as an offering. It's as if the first thought on his mind when the firstborn comes is that he must give thanks to God for giving him this animal.

For Cain, he brings some fruit from the ground to God as his offering. He has toiled and worked this ground which, because of his father, is now hard and unfruitful. He has to spend long hours in scorching sun to get the smallest of crop from it, possibly having to travel long distances to get water to make sure the crop stays alive. He has practically broken his back trying to make sure there will be a crop so he can eat and when it all pays off and there actually is a crop, when his toil and labour has finished and he goes to harvest the crop, his first thought is on all that he has done. He has laboured hard; he has put all the work in; he has worked from early in the morning to late at night. His first thought is not on God, God didn't toil and labour to make this grow and so when it comes to an offering, Cain takes some of the fruit, maybe some that he'd picked at the start of the day and gives it to God as an offering. He recognises that he has to give something and so he gives some fruit.

At a surface level there's maybe not much difference, both give something as a sacrifice and anyway, surely it shouldn't matter what they give, surely giving should be enough.

Yes.

It doesn't matter what they gave, but it does matter how they gave it.

That's why God has regard for Abel and his offering, it was given out of joy, it was given because it was the first thing on Abel's mind. Cain gave because he felt he had to, he knew that he had to give something so he gave some fruit.

This is the first story we read in God's new creation.

After the perfection of the garden had been destroyed, God had hoped that He could still draw alongside this family, that He could still know them and they would be central to this new creation, but here in this first story it seems like not everybody wants to know Him. In fact, if this is the start of what God is hoping will be a new creation and a new relationship with this family it goes from bad to worse in the next few verses.

It seems there was a fallout from the offerings and when the two are in the fields together Cain kills Abel.[9]

Out of nowhere, well maybe out of God's response to each of their offerings, Cain can't stand his brother any longer and decides that the only way to find favour for his offerings, or the only way to find favour with God, or perhaps he wants to have the flocks instead because they found favour with God – for whatever reason, he kills Abel.

This creation, this relationship with this family really isn't going well.

As the story goes on we see something quite familiar.

God speaks to Cain and asks where his brother is, much like He did when He was trying to find his parents in the garden. Cain responds that he doesn't know, not realising that God knows exactly where Abel is and as a result of this act, and possibly even his deviousness, God puts a curse on Cain, driving him out as a fugitive and a wanderer on the earth.

This is all very familiar.

We have heard this story before.

Different character but the same plot.

As this story ends, the next thing we come to is something that tends to put people off the Bible, unless you're one of those people who love a good genealogy!

When Adam had lived 130 years, he fathered Seth …[10]

When Seth had lived 105 years, he fathered Enoch …[11]

When Enoch had lived 90 years, he fathered Kenan …[12]

And so it goes on.

And on.

And man, did they live for a long time; their diet must've been pretty good!

But at the end of this family tree we come to a man called Noah, you might have heard of him.

This man got his name because 'out of the ground that the Lord has cursed, this one shall bring us relief from our work and from the painful toil of our hands'.[13]

He was a hoped-for man who would restore this creation that was broken and cursed, and make it right again. He would free these people from their hardship, from the toil that they had as a result of what had gone on before; the curse that had been placed on the earth by Adam and Eve,[14] and also by Cain.[15]

It was hoped that through being expelled from the garden, Adam and Eve and their family would be the start of a new creation, a new beginning but that hadn't turned out as God had hoped. In fact, we're told just how bad things are in this creation in the next chapter of Genesis when God looks on the earth and saw that 'the wickedness of man was great in the earth, and that every intention of the thoughts of his heart was only evil continually'.[16]

Things were really not how God had hoped.

Things had only become worse.

And then in that very moment they get even worse.

God was sorry that He had made the earth.[17]

After all we've said before, about how God knew His creation was perfect, about how He'd seen beauty and life and joy in it. He had taken pleasure in creating it, and had spent time and energy in making it beautiful. He had seen it all unfold before His eyes and sat back after each day's work was done and said it was good. He had created man, in His image as the pinnacle of this creation and set him in the midst of it to tend and care for it, but now, man, who

He had made, had ruined and broken it and God was sorry He made the earth.

Utterly amazing.

And devastating.

It seems things had got to such a low point, things had been ruined and broken and destroyed to such an extent that God could no longer see any beauty or life or joy in it and the only thing to do was to destroy it.

But there was one thing that saved it.

There was one man who saved it.

And his name was Noah.

While God looked on this creation with regret, He saw one man who found favour with him,[18] who was a righteous man, and blameless in his generation, who walked with God.[19] In the midst of all this darkness was a flicker of light; in the midst of all this brokenness and decay was a sign of life.

Of hope.

And his name was Noah.

This was the man that God hoped would make this creation *tob* once again, who would free it from the curse and start things over. His name suggested it after all and so God gives him plans to build an ark.

Yes, an ark.

Detailed, complicated, planning-permission-pending plans for an ark.

This is the way God is going to redeem and reclaim His creation and it's not pleasant. Ironically it has been the subject of children's songs for years, because the outcome and the reality of what happens is not the kind of material you would choose if you were writing children's books or songs; it's not quite your typical Pixar movie.

Noah builds the ark according to the plans and measurements God has given him, and he takes with him all the animals in their pairings as God told him to. So Noah at the ripe of age of six hundred boards the ark with his family and all the animals.

Seven days later the rain starts.

And keeps going.

And going.

And going.

A bit like what we're used to in Northern Ireland:

For forty days and nights, raising the ark from its place until it floated on the water which kept rising until we're told that it covered the mountains.

Up until this point you can see why it would make a half decent children's book or story but then there's one detail that is included:

Everything that was left behind died.

Now all those children who have heard the story are crying.

God starts over.[20]

Again.

Once again, this story sounds very familiar.

God reclaims this creation so it can be *tob* once again through Noah, and makes a covenant, an agreement with him that He will never again curse the ground because of man.

God tells them something that He has said before, like He told Adam and Eve, He tells Noah to be fruitful and multiply and fill the earth.[21]

God is starting over.

Again.

But as we have seen with the stories from before, things do not always turn out as God had hoped. The people that God had put His trust in do not always turn out as hoped and these stories have started to repeat and repeat, and Noah's story is no exception because in his story there is also division. No one kills anybody else but through the actions of one brother, as noble as they might have been, he finds himself cut off from his brothers and cursed by his father Noah.

A family torn apart, this time by its father.

Separated.

Divided.

And just in time, there comes another genealogy.

Hurray!

This one, however, doesn't end with a hero, it doesn't end with a Noah who is promised to bring relief, or with a hero to save the day; nope, it ends with the clans of the sons of Noah spread all over the earth with one language and the same words.

This may seem a pretty good thing, in fact it may seem an excellent thing and exactly what God wanted for His creation; I mean, if everyone talked in the same way and communicated with the same words they have carried out what God wanted and filled the earth. This has even produced a kind of technological revolution because they're able to produce building materials using brick for stone and bitumen for mortar. The email may not exist yet but for their time they're pretty well advanced!

As a result of this technological revolution they build a city and a tower (Tower of Babel) with its top in the heavens.[22]

It seems this building project is well on its way when God pays it a visit; coming down to see what all the fuss is about (Its top obviously didn't reach that high!), He sees that this is not for His glory, this is not an offering for Him but this is the start of a slippery slope from *tob* to brokenness.

What God had thought would be a new start, a new creation, has begun to decay once again and so He scatters these nations, confusing their language so they can't understand each other.

This genealogy doesn't end with a hero but with a tower that spells disaster.

Once again, this is all very familiar.

This slide from a creation that is *tob* to brokenness rings out as we read.

The same things over again.

Different character but the same plot.

It's almost like a vicious circle.

A story deemed to repeat itself.

A cycle.

It is a cycle, and it's a cycle that continues throughout the whole Bible.

This is how it goes:

God creates a relationship with a person or with a group of people.

The relationship flourishes for a while and the person or people enjoy God's blessing and all that goes with it.

The person or people, they become bored, numb to the blessing and numb to the relationship and start to wish that they had things their own way.

They rebel.

They are disobedient.

They have their own plans.

They cannot get away with their disobedience as it comes at a price.

They are cursed.

In the midst of their curse, in whatever form that comes, God remembers how much He loves them, how He made a relationship with them and so tries to restore this relationship with them and take away the curse.

God is reunited with them.

The relationship flourishes for a while and the person or people enjoy God's blessing and all that goes with it.

The person or people, they become bored, numb to the blessing and numb to the relationship and start to wish that they had things their own way.

They rebel.

They are disobedient.

They have their own plans.

They cannot get away with their disobedience as it comes at a price.

They are cursed.

In the midst of their curse, in whatever form that comes, God remembers how much He loves them, how He made a relationship with them and so tries to restore this relationship with them and take away the curse.

God is reunited with them.

The relationship flourishes for a while and the person or people enjoy God's blessing and all that goes with it.

The person or people, they become bored, numb to the blessing and numb to the relationship and start to wish that they had things their own way.

This cycle goes on and on, repeatedly through the Bible and like all cycles it seems to have no end and no escape.

But God is God and so He continually tries to break this cycle, in the hope that this creation can be made *tob* again.

In the Bible, and in the next chapters we will see how He gets on.

Wooden Ships and Scalpels

CHAPTER THREE

U sually in a generation there is one major film that will define all that generation does. There will be sayings and quotations from it that people will take on as their own language; there will be mannerisms and fashion styles that will mark the 'cool' from the 'not quite so cool'; there will be names that will appear on top baby name lists for some time.

If this occurs more than once a generation, that generation is truly blessed.

One example of this recently would be *Anchorman: The Legend of Ron Burgundy*, a story, surprisingly, about a news anchorman for a TV channel in San Diego during the seventies. People maybe didn't take on the fashion styles quite so much but the sayings and quotations still linger in conversations that you'll hear today. Most people will have seen it, and I say most because anybody who hasn't is generally looked at with a sense of awe, they must have been on the moon or somewhere equally distant from reality!

I even know of one guy who following the film got a tattoo of an old wooden ship on the inside of his bicep. (For those of you who have been on the moon, this is the explanation Ron gives to his friends as to what the word 'diversity' means, citing that he believes it to be an old wooden ship that was used during the Civil War era.)

It defined a generation.

There are many films through the years that have done exactly the same thing, and if you're totally lost when it comes to *Anchorman*, some others might trigger memories for you that are buried somewhere deep down.

For some it was *The Graduate*, for others it might have been *Star Wars* or *The Breakfast Club* or maybe even *This Is Spinal Tap*.

I grew up hearing about all these films and many more, but for different generations they were defining moments, moments that caused a shift in the way they would think, act, speak or even dress.

If I go back a little further in my generation, the *Austin Powers* movies did exactly that. For years on end one of my friends would quote continuously from the films and his responses would incite him to dance like Austin and then fall about laughing – at himself.

If we go back earlier again, we get to another iconic film which made every young guy want to be a fighter pilot and every girl want to marry Tom Cruise.[23]

The film, of course, was *Top Gun*.

Cruise played the cocky fighter pilot 'Maverick' who went to 'Top Gun', the academy for the top pilots in the air force, and the film followed the antics and trials that he went through during his time there and in a subsequent war. It meant that every guy promptly went out and bought aviator shades, sang 'You've Lost That Loving Feeling' and the Jerry Lee Lewis classic 'Great Balls of Fire' to girls in bars and shouted about the 'need for speed' anytime they went near their bicycle or car – none of us could afford F-14s at that point of our teenage years.

These were all classics during my younger years and when I think back there are quite a few more that are ingrained in my memory, but there is one in particular that sticks out for me, stored away and referred to quite often, one which I can't remember a lot of lines from but its name and the broad plot comes back frequently especially if my days start to feel the same:

Groundhog Day.

It was a film made completely by the comedy genius of Bill Murray, who was a reporter sent by his news station to Pennsylvania to cover the annual Groundhog Day on 2 February. While he is there, Bill's character finds himself in a time loop in which he is destined to relive Groundhog Day over and over and over. The film follows him over the repeating day and we discover that the only way he is able to break the time loop is by doing nice things and eventually getting the girl to fall in love with him.

I love this film.

It is also a film that I think about when I read my way through these stories in the Bible as I can imagine God, with the humour and wit of Bill Murray wondering to himself if he is stuck in some kind of Groundhog Day that is doomed to repeat itself over and over in a time loop with the only difference being the characters and their actions.

That is what we have seen so far; this cycle repeating itself over and over with no end in sight, even when we hope that each new time will be different.

So far it is not.

These stories so far may prove that the cycle is still going but to skip the huge chunk that is left of the Old Testament would leave out two characters that are hugely important to all that comes later.

The first is a man called Abram.

As soon as the tower of Babel appears and God scatters and confuses the people, we are introduced to Abram who came from a line of travellers. His father, Terah, took Abram and his brother and their wives and was making his way towards a land called Canaan when they stopped and settled on the way. But it seems God did not want this unscheduled stop and appears to Abram and gives him a promise:

'Go ... and I will make of you a great nation, and I will bless you and make your name great, so that you will be a blessing ... and in you all the families of the earth shall be blessed.'[24]

Although these are not the sort of words we have heard God speak to any individual so far, we can see similarities in them. It seems God wants to use Abram to break this cycle that we have seen repeating; anytime He has approached and spoken to anyone it is for this reason. So these words take on a new meaning for us all as we read them, they become filled with hope and expectation, could this be the man?

It is interesting to note, and to remind ourselves, that none of these men would have known God previously. They wouldn't have a Bible, they wouldn't go to church every Sunday, they wouldn't go to a prayer meeting or house group or anything; the first time they experience or know anything about God is when He speaks directly to them. So, for them, the journey that they embark upon, and all that follows is God revealing Himself to them and them discovering more of who He is. It's no wonder then that they move so quickly and obey so diligently, they experience God directly and that is so overwhelming and inspiring that they do whatever they're asked.

When God speaks to Abram here, He asks him to leave everything behind, leave this country you know, leave your clan or tribe behind and all your father's house and come with me.[25]

This wasn't a simple 'come with me this Sunday to church and then you can go home after', this was a 'give up everything and follow my leading'. In this day and age people travelled in these tribes for safety, for their welfare, they were like a travelling town; if somebody went out on their own how would they survive? How would they tend their flocks and grow crops at the same time? How would they fight off the animals that would come to kill their flocks? How would they survive?

And yet God comes and speaks to Abram and he went.

He dropped everything and went.

He left behind security.

He left behind safety.

He left behind his friends.

And he went.

Into the unknown.

Because God had spoken to him.

And everybody else thought he was crazy.

He went, and his brother went with him along with their wives and their possessions and some of their people. No matter how many you took with you, you were still taking a risk; if you went by yourself you were pretty quickly deemed to die; if you took some people with you, that chance might decrease slightly, the more people the greater the chance of your survival. We aren't told how many Abram took with him, but we are told he went and it seems it didn't take him much time to decide!

So they set off, without a destination in mind, which is kind of how these people worked, and headed in the general direction of Canaan which is where they had set off for with their father. When they reach there, God appears to them and reminds them of the promise He had already given, that He will give this land that they stand looking over to Abram's offspring.

Once again, God is looking for someone to start over with.

In the garden, and in the flood, God had been looking for someone to start over again with and to enjoy his perfect creation with. Each time it had failed, but each time God had not given up and so once again we hear this promise and these words from God as He hopes to start over, this time with Abram.

This time, however, He is in no hurry.

Yes, Abram has been promised children.

Yes, he has been told that the earth will be filled through him.

His offspring will be *that* many.

But Abram is getting old.

With every year that goes by his hope fades.

Was he mistaken?

Did he mishear?

Was all this some kind of cosmic joke?

So he calls out after all this time.

From his confusion.

From his despair.

From his anger.

And is told to go outside.

Not 'go outside you've done something wrong', but told to step outside his tent and look towards the stars in the sky.

Count them.

For that will be the number of your offspring.[26]

From his confusion and despair and anger, Abram still questions and so God makes a covenant with him as a symbol of this promise.

We have seen this word once already when God tried to start again through Noah. The covenant God made with him was that there would never again be a flood to destroy the earth,[27] and again we see a covenant being made here, but what exactly is that?

What does this word 'covenant' mean?

The Hebrew word for covenant is *berit*, which is used to describe an agreement or relationship put in place by God and between Him and His people. When it is used it, it most always is initiated by God and is maintained and fulfilled by Him alone but involves a commitment from both parties along the way.

Only God can set it in place.

Only God can set it in motion.

Only God can keep it going.

Only God can fulfil its promise.

But it requires something from the other party.

For Abram, this *berit* was set in place by God and was a promise that his offspring would be *that* many, as many as the stars of the sky.

In the midst of all the questions that Abram has, God makes this *berit* that it is true.

It will happen.

His offspring will be *that* many.

Despite all his thoughts and frustrations and confusion and despair and anger, God has made this covenant with him to show He's being serious and to remind Abram that's He is being serious, Abram must do something too.

So, to act as a reminder of this *berit*, of what it involves and of the agreement that was made, Abram is to change his name to Abraham and then there's one other thing:

Circumcision.

Yes, I winced too.

This is to be a reminder, and a painful one at that, of this *berit* that has been made between God and Abram. For the generations to come, they are all to be circumcised to remind them that they are included in, and part of, the fulfilment of this *berit*.

But one other thing first.

Before this story about Abram's inability to walk for a few days, there comes a strange twist that you would think would knock everything off track again, but somehow it doesn't.

After God has taken Abram outside and shown him the stars of the sky and reminded him of his promise, and made this *berit* with him, Abram's wife comes up with an idea.

This sounds familiar.

This may be the same story with different characters again.

Abram's wife has not been able to have children and so when they hear of God's promise to make Abram's children as many as the stars in the sky, they do what we would all do.

They doubt.

Even though they've been reminded and have a *berit* with God, which is something only God can fulfil, they doubt and they think that maybe they have to do something into the deal.

So Sarai, Abram's wife, comes up with an idea and seems convinced that the only way that this *berit* will be fulfilled will not be through her but through another woman, and so she gets Abram to sleep with one of servants.

To us, this seems ridiculous.

We know what God means because we know the story, and so we are shouting at the page to tell her and Abram to stop.

But remember.

This is their journey with God.

They haven't known or experienced him before now and so they're getting to know him.

This is the dating stage.

So they assume that if they haven't been able to have children up until this point, then things aren't going to change now.

They're normal people.

Who get confused.

And become misguided.

And who fumble their way with God.

And even laugh at the suggestion of anything else, even if it is from God.[28]

But God, who knows all this and who hasn't spelt out how He's going to fulfil this *berit*, does not deal harshly with them but reminds them of their agreement and spells out that Abram's offspring will come through Sarai.

But there are stipulations.

They must do something too.

And so at the ripe old age of ninety-nine Abram and Sarai change their names and Abram changes something else too.

Along with him, he takes all those who have been born in his house, including the son by Sarai's servant, and has them circumcised as well.

I'm sure they were grateful.

The result, however, is worth it as one year later Abraham and Sarah conceive and give birth to a baby boy called Isaac.

Imagine the joy over that child who was promised to them.

Imagine their joy filled with complete shock that it actually happened to them as God said.

Imagine the party.

And imagine the scene when God comes to Abraham and asks him to offer this only son as a burnt offering.

That might mean nothing to you, but in these days of Abraham that is how they gave thanks, this all acted as part of their worship just like Cain and Abel back at the start. Their worship involved sacrifice and offering, now so did Abraham's.

Imagine that conversation he must've had with Sarah.

Either he didn't have it, or it went extremely well because Abraham gets up early the next morning, saddles his donkey and heads off with Isaac and some men. After three days of travelling they reach the place where they are to make their offering and so Abraham and Isaac go alone up the mountain. When they reach the place, Abraham builds the altar, takes the wood and then ties up his son.

Abraham ties up his son.

His promised heir.

The first of his offspring.

Either he was completely insane or he had some serious conversations with God that we don't know about.

Maybe this is the final stipulation in the *berit* that Abraham has to make.

Whatever it was, he ties Isaac up and puts him on the altar and lifts a knife to strike through his chest when a voice calls out to him to stop, for now it has become obvious that he fears God.[29]

That's a strange word to use:

Fear.

You would think Isaac would be the one with the fear right now – but Abraham?

This isn't a complete fear that comes from being frightened by some sort of wild animal or the fear you get when you're about to jump out of a plane. This fear is purely the type of fear and awe that would make up the normal reaction you would have if you were confronted by God Himself. It carries in it a sense of being frightened, but also a sense of awe and sheer reverence that God Himself has been revealed.

In this case, God now knows that Abraham has fear and awe that makes the ludicrous sound right, and demands that you carry it out when it comes from his mouth.

So when God asked him to kill his own son, born by his wife who hadn't been able to bear any children their whole life, this seems right and seems like the only course of action for Abraham to take.

That's what it is to have fear of God.

It seems this is the final test.

God now has someone who He can start over with, and so He blesses him and confirms that all the nations of the earth will be blessed because Abraham obeyed his voice.[30]

This blessing will make creation *tob* once again.

So it still seems as Abraham lives out his final years in God's blessing and as his number of offspring continues to increase, even as he takes another wife who gives birth to more children. The *berit* that God had put in place with him is being fulfilled as each generation gives birth to another, however, there are hints that all is not as *tob* as it should be. Abraham gives all that he has to Isaac his son, but also gives gifts to the sons of his concubines and as he does this he sends them eastward. To somebody jumping in on the story at this point, this little detail may not seem much, but to us, who have been following God's movements and workings in this creation of His, we see that a little detail like this says a lot more than we would expect.

The first time we heard words like these was back in the garden.

When Adam and Eve took the fruit from the tree, they were driven out from the garden to the East and a flaming sword was placed at the East of it to guard the way back to the tree.[31]

When Cain killed his brother Abel he was sent away from the presence of God and settled in the land of Nod, which was East of Eden.[32]

These little details tell us something about what was going on. Each time East is mentioned, it is not good, something bad was going on, something that went against the *tob* that God had intended for creation.

So when we see this line appear in the story of Abraham, the alarm bells start ringing. Something bad is going on here, something that goes against what God was trying to do in this creation. In whatever way God had hoped to make things right and *tob*, this little hint tells us that there is an undercurrent at work.

With that in mind, the story goes on and at the ripe old age of 175 Abraham dies and was gathered to his people.[33]

Abraham dies not having seen the fulfilment of the *berit* that had been made between him and God, but all is not lost as because of his obedience, the blessings and the offspring that were promised to him are passed on to Isaac.[34]

Although his wife was also barren and unable to have children, Isaac cries out to God who hears his prayer and his wife, Rebekah, like Sarah, becomes pregnant with twins.

This story of Abraham's offspring who became known as the Israelites, continues throughout the story of the Old Testament and it is these people that God fulfils his *berit* through. It is these people that know the blessing of God, but from the moment this *berit* was made with Abraham there are stipulations and requirements and the story of the Old Testament follows how God relates to this people in the middle of fulfilling the deal.

While He tries to make things *tob* again.

It is not an easy story.

There have been undercurrents that we have seen already while Abraham was still alive and even after his death, as his blessings have been passed on to Isaac, and as Isaac becomes the holder of the *berit*, more undercurrents appear.

Even before her children come from her womb, Rebekah inquires of God and is told that within her are two nations, from whom the people will be divided.[35]

Division.

From Cain and Abel.

To Noah.

And now to Abraham's family.

Divided.

Torn apart.

Two nations at war.

The undercurrents are getting stronger.

The cycle is still repeating.

And Abraham knew it.

While God was making this *berit* with Abraham, He made him fall into a deep sleep, and while he was in it, God told him a story about what would happen.

That story was beginning to take shape.

It was beginning to unfold.

It was a story about a people.

A divided people.

A people who would come from Abraham.

It was the story of the cycle.

Remember How It Goes?

CHAPTER FOUR

I'm sure that every once in a while you have one of those dreams that seems so real that when you wake up you're either glad that it's over or you're gutted because you realise it's not real. The last one I remember, I was in the airport in Belfast waiting to get on a plane to America and was chatting away to some people in the departure lounge. As I was just about to board the plane I woke up and it took me a few minutes to realise what was going on and that I was not getting on a plane to go anywhere! For a good part of that day I was still gutted because I wasn't getting on any plane at all, it was all just a dream. Thankfully it doesn't really happen with nightmares but I'm sure the feeling can be equally as real.

When Abraham wakes from his deep sleep I wonder what he must've felt.

He has made this *berit* with God and when he is placed into this deep sleep God tells him that his offspring will be travellers and wanderers in a land that is not theirs and will find themselves in slavery for four hundred years. They will not be slaves forever though, and God will rescue and deliver them from their slavery.[36]

If you had a dream like that it could go either way, it could be one of those dreams that you easily forget, or it could be the one that always flickers in your mind no matter how much time has passed.

This dream was about the cycle.

It was set to continue.

The undercurrents would grow.

This dream would come true.

Even though God has made this *berit* and promised that Abraham and Sarah's offspring would be as numerous as the stars in the sky, it seems that He knew the other side of the deal as well.

God knew about the cycle.

He knew what was going to happen.

That it was going to continue.

That in itself is astounding, the fact that God knew and kept going. It just shows how much He loved, and loves, this creation. He didn't want to give up on what He had created. He doesn't want to throw it away and discard it and start over again, but He wants to make it right, to renew it and redeem it and see it *tob* once again, even though He knows how much that will take.

And it will take a lot.

It will take a lot of time.

A lot of heartache.

A lot of twists and turns.

And a lot of people.

It takes the death of Abraham.

A lot of time passing.

And his dream coming true.

Abraham doesn't see the promise fulfilled, but he doesn't see his dream fulfilled either, a dream which sees his people, the Israelites, wander and end up under the whip of Pharaoh in Egypt.

His offspring are *that* many but they are slaves.

Making bricks.

And mortar.

Working in the fields each day for Pharaoh.

Things are not as they should be.

They are not *tob*.

These people that God wanted for Himself, that He called to be his own, to represent him on earth and worship him and enjoy the relationship that Adam and Eve did, find themselves in the middle of the cycle.

Afflicted.

Tortured.

Beaten.

Bruised.

Broken.

This is not the way it should be.

This is not how they should be living.

They don't deserve this.

And so they cry out.

We have seen this all before, we have heard the cries of people towards God and we have seen God answer them in the midst of their cries.

And He does it again.

Even though the cycle continues and God knows what is to come and how the story unfolds He cannot leave them there in the midst of this slavery and so He does what He always does, He steps in and answers their cries through a man called Moses.

Moses was not a perfect man, he was already guilty of murder by this time[37] and so you might think this wouldn't be the ideal candidate for the job, but God thought otherwise.

This is the man God wants to use to free His people, to lead them away and to fulfil the *berit* he had made.

Moses would not only free them, but lead them to the land Abraham had been promised,[38] a land that would be flowing with milk and honey.[39] These images may not conjure anything for us today, in fact it all seems very *Charlie and the Chocolate Factory*, but for these people who lived day in, day out in slavery, who had nothing, who worked to the bone, these images were things that meant blessing, joy and tranquillity. It wasn't literally that the rivers would be full of milk, full-fat for some and semi-skimmed for the health concious and honey from the sap of the tree; it meant that they wouldn't lack for anything, the things they wouldn't be able to afford or even contemplate eating or drinking while they were slaves in Egypt would be provided by God in abundance in this land.

So Moses sets about freeing the slaves.

Which makes it sound easier than it was.

It involved a lot of negotiating, a lot of bargaining, some grumbling and complaining, a stick that could turn into a snake, the ability to turn water into blood, a lot of frogs, a lot of gnats, even more flies, the death of a lot of animals, skin breaking out into boils, Hollywood hail the size of footballs, locusts that covered every inch of ground, the ability to turn the sky dark and then the death of all the firstborn in every Egyptian family in the land.

Just the usual party tricks then.

These things only happened to the Egyptians and not to the Israelites, and some of them were so horrendous that the Egyptians were crying out to their leader, Pharaoh, to send the Israelites away so they would end, but Pharaoh stood firm until his own firstborn was killed. Then it was time to get rid of these slaves.

For the Israelites, because they weren't affected by any of this, it meant that God had heard them and it meant they gained their freedom, it even meant that as they left the Egyptians were so glad to see them go that they gave them whatever they asked. When all this happened, it was exactly how Abraham had dreamt, his dream coming true.

This day was a celebration, a feast that meant they were free and on their way to the Promised Land, and it became an annual commemoration, remembered and celebrated even to this day, called the Passover.[40]

But because you have read this far, and you know what has been happening so far in this story, you may have guessed what is going to happen next. Things haven't run that smoothly so far, the story

REMEMBER HOW IT GOES?

hasn't been one of happy ever after so I'm sure you're rolling your eyes and getting ready, because, yes, the cycle continues.

It's getting quite annoying now, isn't it?

It just keeps going round.

You would think these people would've learnt by now, but they haven't, and given that the journey to the Promised Land, which is a geographical area, should've taken them around four days, somehow it takes forty years to make this journey.

Four days.

Turned into forty years.

All because of this cycle.

All because they disobeyed.

Remember how it goes?

God creates a relationship with a person or with a group of people.

The relationship flourishes for a while and the person or people enjoy God's blessing and all that goes with it.

The person or people, they become bored, numb to the blessing and numb to the relationship and start to wish that they had things their own way.

They rebel.

They are disobedient.

They have their own plans.

They cannot get away with their disobedience as it comes at a price.

They are cursed.

In the midst of their curse, in whatever form that comes, God remembers how much He loves them, how He made a relationship with them and so tries to restore this relationship with them and take away the curse.

God is reunited with them.

And so it continues even before a day passes.

As God led them up out of Egypt by a pillar of cloud in the day and fire by night,[41] avoiding territory that He knew might frighten them, they came to their first problem, a rather large problem and a rather watery problem.

The Red Sea.

While they were looking over this vast sea and wondering how this was going to work out, they suddenly became very aware of noise, specifically the noise of horses and chariots and of an army marching. It turns out Pharaoh had changed his mind about letting them go, possibly when he realised that his entire workforce had walked out of the country, so he set out to pursue these slaves and bring them back, and it didn't take long until he found and trapped them at the edge of the Red Sea.

An army on one side is never nice to meet, but an army on one side with a sea on the other is even more unpleasant and so the Israelites cried out asking why God and Moses had brought them here to die.

I'm sure you can understand their reason to cry, it seems pretty plausible to me, but they are reminded that once again they will see God at work; they had seen it so many times before in Egypt and now they will see it again.

And so Moses produces another party trick.

God tells him to walk to the Sea and lift his staff.

So Moses walks to the sea and lifts his staff.

And parts the sea.[42]

As you do.

What seems so improbable to us is now becoming the usual for these people and God is showing them once again that He is serious about His *berit* that He made with Abraham.

Without going into the detail, and I don't think this has been made into a children's song yet, to further show His strength and power, and His protection over this group, He closes over the sea on the advancing army.

Their journey towards their Promised Land continues with that fear that brings awe and reverence, but also for them brings a confidence that God is with them.

Or so you would think.

Sometimes it doesn't take much to pick out the really enthusiastic and passionate people, the people who will take any task big or small and run with it, and similarly it doesn't take much to pick out the grumblers and complainers, those people who don't want to do anything much.

I have been on various mission teams over the years and everybody loves a good mission team. Getting to go away to a far-flung part of the world is exciting and exhilarating. I went on a team like that to Western Africa, which went to build a bridge across a river allowing a whole community to cross it at this point rather than having to travel an extra eight hours to get to the nearest town. As we landed in the dilapidated airport and drove the many hours to get to the village, I can still remember the houses along the roads that were in complete darkness because they couldn't afford electricity, or they simply didn't have the means to get access to it. More than that, I remember crossing the river standing on an old US Army lorry and driving into the village for the first time to see these people living in circular mud huts with a few of them standing outside cooking a goat on a spit.

Everybody loves those sort of experiences.

Being able to make a real change somewhere like that.

Being able to get involved.

I've also been on mission teams to the South of Ireland, to a ministry that my sister and her husband run from the city of Cork. To them and myself, that is as much of a mission, but often I have found that when I go on teams to volunteer with their ministry, that attitude of service and mission can be lost. I'm very quickly able to tell who sees it as a mission and who sees it as a holiday, and I can tell which ones to send to clean out the toilets, and which ones will only want to sit around chatting to their friends and drinking lattes.

No matter what situation you are in, you can always tell who the glass-half-full people are, the people who will see the potential in everything and put up their hand and act on anything, and you can always tell who the glass-half-empty kind of people are, the ones who will keep their head down and grumble no matter where you are and no matter what you're doing.

Those glass-half-empty people are usually forgetful people.

Maybe not in the short-term memory way, when you walk into a room and can't remember why on earth you're there or what you were going there for, but they were forgetful of what they had been given, of the blessings they have and had, of the ways in which they've come through all that they have.

Glass-half-empty people generally don't focus on the positive outcomes but the negative, that's why they're glass-half-empty people, they see it in a negative way, it's empty; what does cleaning toilets have to do with mission anyway?

It's a shame that from what we see of the Israelites they were a glass-half-empty group, a forgetful, negative bunch and we don't have to travel too much longer before they're at it again.

Three days later, of wandering in the wilderness they had once again forgotten all that God had done for them. They had walked these three days in scorching heat without water and were thirsty, so they complain to Moses. God not only provides water for them to drink, turning bitter water into drinkable water, and then leading them to a desert oasis, but promises them that if they continue to follow Him, He will protect them and keep disease and illness from them.[43]

Once again God hears their cries and provides for them, not only with the basics but lavishly and with more than they could have desired, but they're glass-half-empty people.

As their journey continues and they move further into the wilderness, they begin to forget.

Initially this journey should've taken four days, we're now into a couple of weeks in the wilderness and it seems they've taken a wrong turn somewhere or God is once again taking them the long way for a reason. So, one month and fifteen days of walking later, they are hungry. I would guess they're pretty starving by this point.

I start to get quite grumpy if I miss a few meals so I can imagine they'd be pretty grumpy by this point. So out of that grumpiness they complain to Moses, wishing they'd stayed in Egypt even as slaves, at least there they had meat and bread they could eat until they were full.

Once again God hears their cries and rains bread from heaven.[44]

God once again shows His desire to lavish this people with all that He can, even when they complain and grumble and forget, which they do frequently.

One of the most serious occasions of their forgetfulness, as their journey continues, happens at a place called Mount Sinai.

As God leads them from Egypt towards the Promised Land, it is another new experience for everyone. These generations that are being led have not encountered God before, they have had no access to Him as slaves in Egypt. They have probably heard the stories from their ancestors and know all about God leading Abraham, but they know very little of Him in the everyday.

Now that all has changed.

This God they had heard about, who led their forefather, Abraham, is now leading them in a pillar of cloud by day and a pillar of fire by night.

This is back to the dating stage.

So as God leads them on this journey, He takes them via Mount Sinai where He calls for and meets with Moses to give him what is known as the Ten Commandments.

It's interesting to see how they start.

'I am the Lord your God, who brought you out of the land of Egypt, out of the house of slavery.'[45]

It is not a list of laws for the sake of having some order and making sure God is in control, remember this is the dating stage.

God is saying to this people, remember who I am, I am the one who heard you, who answered your cries, who brought you out of slavery. I am the one you have heard about. You may not know me yet yourself, but this is how you know me.

This is how you get to know me.

These are the things I care about.

For the Israelites this is what they want to know.

Normally people are scared of the gods, modern day films and stories are of the gods who don't want to be known but who come in thunder and lightning to kill and destroy. It's no wonder in ancient times that people were scared of the gods, that they would give anything to please them, to stay on their good side. It's hard to understand, but you can see why people slaughtered their own children so they wouldn't make the gods angry.

These are the types of gods people knew about, not a god that came to them and told them how to relate, who gave them specific ways of knowing exactly what they were about.

God was laying Himself open.

Sharing Himself with them.

Telling them who He was.

But before He even got the chance to finish, the Israelites, who were at the bottom of this Mount, were starting to forget.

Moses had been away for quite some time and so the people began to forget and become impatient, maybe they were hungry or thirsty. Maybe it's because they thought this god had abandoned them and so they tell Moses's assistant to get up and make for them gods who will go before them and lead them.[46]

They carve out of their gold earrings a calf and begin to worship it as the god that brought them out of Egypt and that will lead them on.

They must've been afraid that God had left them.

There must've been another god who would lead them and they had to please it.

So they chose a calf.

This did not go down well and as soon as Moses starts to come down the mountain and he hears the singing and dancing around this calf he loses the plot, grinds up the calf into dust and puts it in the water, forcing the Israelites to drink it.[47]

They might be forgetful, but Moses is not, and God is not. He still remembers the *berit* He made with Abraham, freeing them from their slavery and taking them to be with them in this Promised Land. Even though they grumbled and complained and rebelled and tested the limits and were disobedient, God kept them on their journey, however, there was one slight problem, there was a consequence.

God doesn't forget.

Their complaining and grumbling and rebellion time and time again had reminded God of the past, of the ways in which His creation had been destroyed, of the rebellion that had happened before, of the cycle that kept repeating and so He wanted to start over again to make sure this creation would be *tob*.

To do this God kept them on their journey for forty years.

What should've been four days turned into forty years meaning that those people who had complained and grumbled and rebelled would not see the Promised Land. It didn't mean that no one would ever see it, but that those who were disobedient would die out.[48]

So it takes them a rather long time to get there and forty years later, as they stand on the verge of entering into this land they are given a warning.

If things continue this way, if the cycle continues, there will be blessing and curse.

For us, this is nothing new, we have seen it all unfold before, but God sets it out to these people in no uncertain terms.

If they faithfully obey the voice and the words of God they will be blessed and will be a blessing to other nations.[49]

If they do not faithfully obey the voice and the words of God they will be cursed and will be a horror to the other nations.[50]

These are not easy words to hear.

They are not to be taken light-heartedly.

They are not to be joked about.

Or forgotten.

Or dismissed.

They are serious.

And important.

And as the rest of the story unfolds in the Old Testament we get front row seats to the rest of the journey of this people. We get to see as they grow and expand into a huge nation, we get to see them as they live in the land their forefather Abraham had been promised.

We also get to see how they responded to God's warning.

We get to see the times when God's voice and words are taken seriously and importantly and we also get to see when they are forgotten and dismissed, they are taken lightly and seen as unimportant and the Israelites are cursed.

As they enter into this Promised Land and we go with them through the rest of the Old Testament the story continues.

And so does the cycle.

Question Marks and Pottery

CHAPTER FIVE

So if the whole story of Israel has some light it can shed on today, if it means anything at all; if their story in some way becomes like our story and becomes our story, then surely whatever was said to them, whatever answers they got must be of interest to us?

If this isn't the case we're simply consigned to repeat history over and over again because we will never learn what worked the first time.

In a book of the Bible which is called Ecclesiastes, the main character, who is known as the teacher, reminds us again and again that nothing is new under the sun,[51] things are going to repeat time and time again, but for some reason we never learn.

Maybe it's because the postmodern mindset holds that we can do whatever we want and so we don't need to learn or listen to anybody else, we can make our own ways and make our own mistakes; so we revolt against anyone and anything that tells us it can teach us or prevent us from making the same mistake. We are now actually told to learn from our mistakes and to go ahead and make them regardless of whether anybody else has already made them.

So we go ahead and make our mistakes and often knowingly, but surely there has to be some other way.

Surely there has to be something that can at least guide us through our lives so the same mistakes do not have to happen again.

There is a mural on the end of a house in Belfast (you can see it on the mural tour) which has a great quote 'those who forget the past are condemned to repeat it'. It's very fitting for Northern Ireland but also fitting for us as well as part of this story.

To realise what has already happened and to know what mistakes not to make we first need to remind ourselves of our own story, the things that make up our lives, the situations we are in and the places we find ourselves.

Many of us find ourselves discontented and unsatisfied.

We know there is more out there somewhere and so we become discontented and disillusioned by what we have here, some call this the grass-is-always-greener syndrome. We want more and more.

Bigger and bigger.

More expensive.

More flashy.

More horsepower than the last one.

More rooms.

Nicer furniture.

More apps.

More battery life.

More zeroes on the end of the pay cheque.

Then when we turn on the news or look on the internet we see that this is not what everybody wants because some people simply want water or food for that day and that makes us think.

In fact you don't have to look too far around you to see something that is not the way it should be in this world.

Something that is out of sync.

Something that is out of balance.

Something that has gone wrong.

It may be in our own lives or the life of someone we love dearly. You may be saying those things, and if you're not, I challenge you to talk to the people around you, talk to your own family and find out what they're asking.

Where was God when this happened to me?

Why did my father die?

Why did he have to die so young of cancer?

Why did my mother have to look after him for so long?

Why did my sister hang herself?

Why is my daughter cutting herself?

Why did my husband run off with another woman?

Why can I not afford to send my children to school with a lunch?

Why do I not know where the next month's rent will come from?

Why did I lose another job?

All these questions and so many more run through the minds of individuals and whole families in our society today. There is no use in imagining that it does not go on because it does. If you don't realise that you are blinding yourself to the reality of the world around you, wrapping yourself in a little bubble, maybe to hide yourself from real life, or maybe because you're scared to really embrace the mess and the hurt that's going on around you.

To do that is dangerous because when something happens in your own life, when something goes wrong or tragedy strikes the chances are your whole world will implode around you. I'm sure you have seen it happen to someone else whose world has collapsed when they have lost a loved one or had bad news themselves.

To deny these things will happen is disastrous, it is dangerous, it is unhealthy.

Maybe it's because you think it will never happen to you or because you think it shouldn't happen to you.

This world in which we inhabit is the most technologically advanced world in human history. It has every kind of gadget and device you can think of; it has planes, trains and automobiles; it has the internet and multiple ways of communicating; it has made advances in the last ten years that never could have been imaginable and it doesn't look like it will stop either. Medical technology and success rates are increasing all the time (even though the greatest medical breakthrough was the flushing toilet[52]) and so maybe for all these reasons we think we will be fine, that these advances will be good enough to keep us alive.

The worlds in which we work have dramatically changed as well.

We now work in multimillion, if not billion, turnover companies; everybody is dealing in tens and hundreds of thousands and if you're not you're deemed a failure. I often walk through the streets of Belfast and frequently I overhear business men and women talking about deals they have been doing that day for hundreds of thousands and millions of pounds. Years ago you would have been laughed at for even thinking in those numbers.

Maybe these people think they are too important to get sick or ill, or lose their jobs.

For most of us, however, we can see what is really going on; we can see the heartache and the hurt that goes on around us, whether it's out in the open or behind closed doors.

And for most of us, that hurts.

That causes us to ask questions.

That stirs us and moves us.

That takes us back to the story of Israel.

In all of the parts of the story we've looked at there has been suffering and there has been hurt; people have been crying out and people have been questioning all that has been going on around them and all the circumstances they find themselves in.

In the story of the Garden of Eden although we do not hear them asked directly, we can see how both Adam and Eve would think:

'Why did I do that?'

'Why did I let her deceive me?'

'Why did God let this happen to us?'

'Why didn't we get another chance?'

'Why did He have to throw us out?'

'Why didn't He throw the snake out instead of us?'

'Why did He allow the snake to do that to us?'

In the very next chapter of the Bible we see the story of Cain and Abel and in amidst the anger of Cain we can imagine him asking:[53]

'Why did God look on Abel's offering with favour?'

'What was wrong with mine?'

'Why did he become the favourite?'

'Why does he have it made?'

'Why did I do that?'

'Why is his blood crying out?'

In the story of Noah we can imagine Noah asking:

'Why me God?'

'Why are you choosing me?'

'Why are you destroying everything?'

In the story of Abraham

'Why must I kill my son?'

'Surely there has to be another way?'

'I'm too old to do this, you must be wrong God.'

In the story of Egypt, when we find God's chosen people being mistreated and beaten under the captivity of Pharaoh, as they are being made to work longer and longer hours from morning to night, as they are whipped if they take a break, as their children are being massacred, as they realise how far they have fallen, we can imagine them asking:

'Why did this happen, God?'

'Why us?'

'Why are you not doing anything?'

'Where are you?'

'Why are our children being killed?'

'Why won't you do anything?'

'When will we be free from this?'

'When will God rescue us?'

In the story of Moses we see a man who has to guide this people, a people who he hears being calls 'stiff-necked'[54] and in fact it is as if God changes His mind and wants to destroy them from the face of the earth.[55] This is the people Moses has to contend with for forty years and more as they constantly whine and moan their way through the wilderness. You can imagine him asking:

'Why have you done this God?'

'Why have you chosen to afflict me with these people?'

'Why must they be so disobedient?'

'Why do I have to put up with this for forty years?'

'Why didn't you get someone else to do this?'

'Why won't you let me in after all this time?'

'Why have I done this all for nothing?'

On and on go the questions that we find in these stories alone and there are many more that we have not encountered or dealt with on the way. These are left for you to journey through and to find out what questions arise. But there is one story, one person who has questions to ask, that cannot be passed over and that is a story about a man called Job.

This story is debated about and scholarly opinion is wide ranging when it comes to it, but those debates do not matter here for all we want to see is what Job does.

As we read through his story we discover by way of a heavenly dialogue between God and the Accuser, who seems to be there when the angels come to present themselves to God. 'Accuser' is the same type of word that is used about the serpent in the story of Adam and Eve; it can be understood as the evil force which stands against the *tob* of this creation. The Accuser is asked what he has been doing and whether he spotted Job whilst he was on the earth. God is particularly pleased with Job and praises him as being unique upon the earth, describing him as a righteous man, with there being no one on earth quite like him, blameless and upright, who fears God and shuns evil.[56] The question arises about whether Job truly fears God for nothing, with the Accuser claiming he only fears God because he has put a hedge around him, his household and everything he has. The true way to find out whether Job truly fears God is to stretch out His hand and strike everything he has, because then Job will curse God to His face.

With the accusation set, God lets the Accuser have his chance, allowing certain tragedies to overcome Job without Job himself being harmed.

His oxen and donkeys were stolen.[57]

His sheep and servants spontaneously combust.[58]

His camels were stolen and his servants murdered.[59]

His sons and daughters are killed when the oldest brother's house is demolished by wind, while they are inside.[60]

All within a matter of minutes.

This may sound too bizarre all to happen at once, it may be too extreme to even imagine that it was true, but that is what happens to Job and yet he does not curse God.

In fact he states that God gives and takes away, may the name of God be praised.[61]

At this point we return to the heavenly setting where God and The Accuser are once again in dialogue regarding Job. The Accuser claims that once Job's skin is touched then he will curse God to His face and so once again Job is given over for the Accuser to do with him as he pleases.

Job is given painful sores from the soles of his feet to the top of his head and the only relief he seems to get is to scrape himself with a piece of broken pottery which is not something that is advisable in any circumstance.[62]

Through all of this we can only imagine the questions Job may have been asking. Any one of these troubles happening would cause us to crumble, to grieve and cry out but here we have a man who has calamity upon calamity, tragedy after tragedy upon his shoulders and he tears his clothes, he sits in ashes and he scrapes himself with a piece of broken pottery. That really sounds like he is feeling pain; that may even be what happens when someone's world implodes around them without any warning.

His friends try to comfort him.

His friends try to get him to repent for unknown sin.

His friends try to tell him that everything will be ok.

Does that sound familiar?

His wife tells him to curse God and die but Job will not, instead he sits in his ashes and scrapes himself with broken pottery.

Do those questions sound familiar?

Can you imagine being in the same place as Job?

Have you had those things happen to you?

Did you cry out in the same way?

What did you ask God to do?

What did you shout at God?

What have your friends said to you?

The end of the story of Job is one of the most fascinating in the Bible because into this story God Himself speaks with question after question, it seems the tables have turned.

Having been bombarded with question after question by God, Job's only response is to admit that he spoke of things he did not understand[63] and having seen God with his own eyes he admits that the only thing he can now do is despise himself and repent in dust and ashes.[64]

Despise himself?

Now?

After all of those things?

The Hebrew word used here is *maas* which means to become vile or to think of yourself as vile.

This is an interesting way to think.

Job does not despise himself or feel that he is vile due to all that has happened to him. He does not think that he has done anything wrong to warrant these things that have happened to him and so he is safe in his knowledge that there must be something greater at work. When God finishes speaking to him and speaks to his friends he discovers that he in fact has been right, something greater was at work.[65]

As God turned His attention to Job, it seems He was reminding him of exactly who is in charge and it also seems Job got the point pretty quickly, repenting in dust and ashes, despising the fact that he could've or would've thought anything else other than God being at work.

This ending to the book of Job does not mean we cannot ask questions.

It does not mean that we have to sit silently while things fall apart in our lives and despair sets in, that is in fact the most dangerous thing to do. This ending to Job reminds us to keep note of who is really in charge, of what our true position is, of our true dependence on God for all things, and we too should keep hold of that phrase that God gives and He takes away.

Do not let Job make you think you cannot ask questions.

This humble attitude that Job shows is amazing, and is in stark contrast to the attitude of Israel. When we left the story of Israel as they were standing at the edge of the Promised Land about to step into the place they had been promised – a land flowing with milk and honey – we know the cycle will continue. As we journey further through the Old Testament we discover that in the following years nothing changes at all; this obedience and disobedience continues and we see that the cycle does indeed continue. As a people their attitude is not one of humility like Job, but rather they continually forget who they are, what they are supposed to do and what they are supposed to be. This attitude leads to their disobedience and then as the cycle progresses we see that they are questioning and crying out to God as much as they ever have, asking Him where He is; asking Him what He's doing; asking Him why they aren't where they once were because now it seems like God has abandoned them.

In another book, 2 Samuel, the king at the time, a man called David, is bringing the Ark of the Covenant back to Jerusalem after it being in captivity for years. It is interesting to note at this point a few things about the Ark of the Covenant. It was basically a box which contained two stone tablets that the Ten Commandments had been written on when the people of Israel were at Mount Sinai. These were the words etched by God's own finger as He revealed Himself to His people and the Ark was one of the most important pieces of 'furniture' that the Israelites had in their possession. Before that it had been in the possession of the Philistines and later had been at the house of Abinadab for almost a century.

While David was bringing the Ark up to Jerusalem one of the Levites had been struck dead as he touched the Ark and so David and all the people were afraid of it. For this reason he decided that it should not come up to his home but should go to the house of Obed-Edom for three months. While the Ark was there God blessed Obed-Edom and his whole house. As soon as David heard of this blessing he went and took the Ark up to the city of David. It's funny how fear can make us miss out on blessing that comes from God.

With the Ark now in his possession David is promised that his house and his kingdom and his throne will be established forever.[66] As he is giving thanks to God for this, he spells out that the people of Israel were to be the one nation on earth that God went out to redeem as a people for Himself, and to make a name for Himself, and to perform great and awesome wonders by driving out nations and their gods from before his people whom he redeemed from Egypt.[67]

That is what Israel were *supposed* to be, a redeemed people but also a redeemed people who were to be witnesses to the rest of the earth.

That is what they were supposed to be, but as their story continued it turned out they were not the people they were supposed to be.

The cycle continued.

They were silent towards God.

They forget who they were.

Their attitude changed.

They questioned.

Disobedience.

Back to silence.

Back to not hearing God's voice.

Back to not doing what God wanted them to do.

Back to being under the curse.

Back to crying out.

In the midst of these cries, and in the midst of these years of this cycle repeating, we meet an interesting group of people called the prophets. These prophets were generally thought of as a weird and eccentric bunch and would be the type you would cross the street to avoid, but they always came with big news. They came to tell the people why they were in this position, why they weren't hearing from God, why they weren't seeing the blessing that God had in store for them, to remind them of what they have done.

Time after time these people have needed reminders.

Back to Moses and his constant reminders so the people would remember that they had been liberated once before and due to that liberation they should respond in faithful obedience.

Back to the people forgetting and so these prophets came to tell Israel the same thing; to remind them of where they should be, of what they should be doing.

The prophet Jeremiah tells them that God will pronounce His judgements upon them because of their wickedness in forsaking him and burning incense to other gods and worshipping what their hands made.[68]

The prophet Ezekiel is sent by God to a rebellious nation who has rebelled against him, both them and their fathers.[69]

The prophet Zechariah tells the people to return to God, not to be like their forefathers who were told to turn from their evil ways and with whom God was very angry.[70]

The prophet Amos, who prophecies in a time when Israel was successful both materially and politically, tells them that, unless they repent, God will sweep through the house of Joseph like a fire, you who turn justice into bitterness and cast righteousness to the ground, who turn blackness into dawn and darken day into night.[71]

And so they continued to prophecy.

They continued to encourage the people to once again turn to God.

They continued to face opposition and death threats, becoming ostracised and ignored.

And because they didn't listen to these prophets the people of Israel eventually found themselves in a place of exile once again, another form of Egypt, another type of oppression and once again the questions began.

But that was all long ago.

We don't have those problems today.

We don't need to listen to any prophets today.

We have it all sorted out.

We know it all.

Everything's cool.

Really?

We don't need to listen?

These stories have no relevance until you hear the questions they asked, the questions that they cried out, and then you realise:

Their cries mirror your cries.

Their questions mirror your questions.

Their pain mirrors your pain.

Our stories can be projected onto theirs and they fit.

When we realise this, we suddenly understand that we do not stand alone in the present world. Suddenly we realise that there has been a past to the world, we have not just appeared here and now but there have been people who have gone before and people who have made the same mistakes as we have and seen the same consequences as we have.

The Bible is often seen as simply a historical document with no real connection to real life; that somehow the people that it talks about and the stories that it tells are in some other world entirely which has nothing to do with the world that we currently occupy and inhabit. The one thing that corrects that view is pain.

Oppression.

Hurt.

Things that make us question who we are and what we believe.

Things that really matter to us here and now.

When we realise that and understand that, we realise that the Bible deals with those issues, it deals with those questions. We find people who have lost loved ones and whose only form of escape is to sit in a pile of ashes and scrape themselves with broken pottery. We find people who are working non-stop from dawn until dusk to make targets, often having to go in search of materials all the while knowing that if they do not meet their targets they will be whipped and beaten by their employers. We find people who are caught for murder, who have to watch people drown, who have to listen to moaning and complaining day in and day out, we meet a whole range of people who are in trouble and on the run.

When we meet these people, when we hear the stories they have to tell suddenly it comes to life, the whole story takes on a completely new meaning.

If we let it.

The Man Who Had Everything

CHAPTER SIX

I was brought up on the very north coast of Northern Ireland which is a beautiful place to grow up. In the winter there is something idyllic about the quiet streets and the crisp winter days, and in the summer, if you can avoid the tourists that invade those same streets to spend their long-collected 2 ps in the slot machines, there is something even more beautiful about the long evenings that stretch nearly until midnight.

It was on one of those evenings that I remember walking a part of the coastline with my parents as a young boy. We were walking along a stretch of path that only had some rocks between us and the open Atlantic, and as we were walking along my mother, who always has a good eye for nature, spotted a shadow appearing and disappearing out towards the horizon. We stopped to investigate or at least to try to see more clearly and it turned out to be a porpoise, and then it turned out to be several porpoise bobbing about in the evening sun, seemingly enjoying it as much as we were. These animals are a common sight along the coast but for some reason I remember this occasion quite clearly.

As we stood there watching them play in the water I suddenly realised that other people had stopped as well, first to see what we were staring at and then to enjoy this spectacle for themselves.

There were still a lot of people who were making their way along, oblivious to what was going on, or so consumed in their own world that they didn't care, but for the rest of us it was a chance to stop and take part in something amazing.

REMEMBER HOW IT GOES?

What we do here at this point is something similar: stop and see what other people are looking at, because if we don't we may miss out on something quite beautiful that we wouldn't have otherwise noticed ourselves.

To stop and look is a choice.

To pay attention is a choice.

To listen is a choice.

To take heed is wise.

If you do, you might enjoy something new and beautiful.

If you don't, you may never know what you've missed.

It is a choice to realise that those who have gone before actually may have worked some things out, they might have seen that beautiful and profound thing and all they're trying to do is to show you, they may have advice for you just when you need it.

There is a story about a man called Solomon in the Bible, a son of David, the king. When David died God appeared to him in a dream and gave Solomon the chance to ask for anything he would want.

Imagine that moment.

Anything you want.

If you pause for a minute and imagine your response to that question it may surprise you what you would ask for.

It reminds me of a joke about a genie.

You may want answers more than anything else, to all those questions you have, all the questions we asked in the last chapter.

You may want wealth.

Fame.

Fortune.

A big house.

With a pool to match.

You may want millions of pounds.

The magazine headlines.

And column inches.

The status amongst your peers.

You may want to be known.

Or maybe something more simple that Miss World would want, like world peace.

Solomon asks for experience.

Wisdom.

Discernment.

The ability to understand justice.

The ability to administer justice.

They wouldn't have been my first thoughts but they were Solomon's and that is what he receives, in fact it tells us that because of this request and not the request for riches or the death of his enemies God gives him all this and more, promising to make him the most famous man of wisdom so there never has or ever will be anyone like him again.[72]

He goes on to write many wise sayings and the book of the Bible called Proverbs contains a number of these. He is also widely thought to have written the book we mentioned at the start of the last chapter called Ecclesiastes, which is a very different book.

Whereas Proverbs is a book of sayings, Ecclesiastes could be called a book of questions taking the form of a discussion.

This discussion takes place between two voices and in it one of the voices exasperates that everything is meaningless.[73] He is looking at all that is around, everything he has done or carried out, everything he has worked or strived for and after looking at it all, he calls it meaningless.

This is the way we have translated it.

In the original language this word *hebel* can mean a range of words but in this case is translated as 'vanity' or even as 'mist'. You may think that these meanings go against what has been said but all translations of *hebel* brand the related activity, whatever it may be, as worthless or futile, as an activity that disperses and disappears as quickly as breath or mist.

It can now be seen why it is translated as meaningless.

These things, these activities are meaningless because they last as long as your breath does on a cold winter's day, or the mist which falls and disappears.

They are futile.

They disappear.

They vanish.

They are meaningless.

While this voice continues to look at all these works under the sun, this refrain continues to echo and we wonder whether he will ever return to find hope, to find a way out, to find anything that will last or have meaning.[74]

This is the man who had everything.

Wealth.

Fame.

Wisdom.

Notoriety.

And lots and lots and lots of questions.

This story of Solomon reflects that cycle we have seen, circling around and around; that same cycle which we have seen the whole way through the story of Israel.

They had what they wanted.

They were under God's blessing.

They forgot who they were.

They forgot who they were called to be.

They forgot their blessings.

Their attitude changed.

They asked questions.

They were silent towards God.

Disobedience.

Back to silence.

Back to not hearing God's voice.

Back to crying out.

This cycle that we have seen in so many of the stories throughout the Bible continued through generation after generation without exception. There were the prophets who took notice and tried to make people see what was happening, who spoke on God's behalf with God's words to try and get people to realise what was happening but it didn't work, the cycle continued.

It even continued with someone like Solomon, the man who was said to be the most wise and powerful man there ever will be. He even continued the cycle.

It seems there was no one who could break it.

It seems no one wanted to break it.

The cycle continues.

And it still does.

Even to this day.

So we find ourselves in the same position, in the same cycle, in the same story. Just like the people of Israel, we find ourselves in that blank page at the middle of the Bible.

Waiting.

Hanging pregnant with questions.

Loaded with them.

Waiting for answers.

Waiting for something to be done.

For someone to act.

That is what is happening in the blank page in the middle of the Bible, in between the Old and the New Testaments.

All Israel is waiting for answers to the questions that they have had, so we find ourselves too, standing beside them waiting.

The story that we have seen in the first chapters brought us to this point. They walked us through the story of Israel with all its successes and failures, with all its obedience and disobedience, with all its triumphs and trials, but ultimately in that story we are left hanging.

There is no nice ending for it all.

There is no restoration.

There is no happy conclusion.

They are left waiting for a climax to come, for peace to be restored, for a finality to occur, but it does not.

We have walked with them as the cycle has continued time and time again, as they have been disobedient time and time again and so like any cycle, it just keeps on repeating. There does not seem to be any way to stop it.

That is where we last see Israel, in the middle of the cycle.

The last sections of books in the Old Testament are called the Major and Minor Prophets. We have met these prophets before.

They are included in the cycle.

They are part of the cycle.

Their words form these last sections and are words showing how far the people of Israel have gone from their original calling[75] and about what will happen to them if they do not turn back once again.[76]

They also come true.

In the book of Lamentations we see these words have come true, Jerusalem, their home, has been destroyed and looted, God's Holy Temple and their place of worship has been destroyed all as a prophet told them it would happen.

And so they wait.

Feeling hurt.

Abandoned.

But all is not lost.

In these words of the prophets we find a flicker of light because we find words about the steadfast, unmoving love that God has for Israel[77] and the promises that still remain for them in spite of all they have done.[78] We find words about a time when the cycle can stop and all can once again enjoy the riches and blessings of God's covenant.

Their words ring with hope and rejoicing, of one who will come to bring about this time.

Who will come to bring healing.

Who will come to restore.

Who will come to end the cycle.[79]

But they haven't come yet.

This is what Israel is waiting for as we stand beside them on the blank page in the middle of the Bible; and the name for this one who would come, the one they were waiting for, is 'Messiah'.[80]

When we step off that blank page and into the first page of the New Testament we find again something that for us is not very exciting, unless, as we've discovered, you're into that sort of thing: a genealogy.

Abraham was the father of Isaac, and Isaac was the father of Jacob, and Jacob the father of Judah and his brothers, and Judah …

And Perez.

And Hezron.

And Ram.

And on it goes.

But when we look closer and read through to the end of this genealogy we find some interesting words:

'Jacob fathered Joseph the husband of Mary who gave birth to Jesus who is called the Messiah.'[81]

Within a few lines of the opening of the New Testament we have an interesting insight into who these people were claiming this man Jesus was:

Him.

The One.

The One they had talked about.

The One who would come to heal.

The One who would come to restore.

The One who would come to redeem.

The One who would come to end the cycle.

The Messiah.

The One who everybody was standing on the blank page waiting for was here; in the flesh and his name was Jesus.

This was big news.

This was a big claim by this man.

This could be the answer to all those questions.

So, all the expectations that Israel had they were now looking at Jesus to fulfil, and the gospels or the books that were written about him sought and still seek to explore this issue of whether he was or was not the Messiah.

As we read through these books we discover that the claims of Jesus as Messiah were not always met with hope and rejoicing as expected from the words of the prophets.[82] With this time of expectation you would think they would be met with celebration but in fact on many occasions his claims were met with hate and retribution.

That was because this man, who was claiming to be Messiah didn't come as he was expected to.

The Israelite people had certain ideas about what the Messiah would do and although we see that in the first century Jesus met these criteria, he did not meet them in the way that the people were expecting and indeed in the way that they wanted them to be met.

Sure he was using all the right phrases, saying all the right things, doing miraculous things, but was he restoring Israel to her pride and glory?

Not in the way they wanted.

At this time Israel was under the authority of the Romans who had invaded and plundered their land. They had made the Israelites prisoners in their own land. They had made them slaves once again just like they were in Egypt and so as Israel waited on that blank page in the middle of the Bible some of their questions might have been:

When and how will God get rid of these Romans so we can get our Promised Land back?

When will He send someone to lead us out of slavery?

They wanted rid of these Romans.

They wanted their land back.

They wanted their rights back.

They wanted to stop paying taxes to a foreign army.

They wanted the Messiah to set them free.

Just like Moses did.

And so when Jesus came, claiming to be the Messiah this was music to their ears, they were delighted because suddenly there was hope that they would get rid of the Romans and get their religious freedom back, but Jesus didn't do what he was expected to do.

He didn't wave the sword.

He didn't fight.

He didn't take arms.

Or plot schemes to overthrow the Romans and give them back their land.

Instead he brought peace.

He brought love.

He spoke of turning the other cheek.[83]

Of loving your enemies.[84]

Of praying for those who persecute you.[85]

He didn't seem to care for the practices of the teachers of the Law or the scribes and rulers but instead spent time with the tax collectors and prostitutes, the outcasts in society, the very people who lined the Romans' pockets and their own pockets at the same time!

On one occasion as he sat on a mountain and taught all those who gathered around him, he turned the teachings of the day upside down and taught them something new:

Blessed are the poor in Spirit.

Blessed are those who mourn.

Blessed are the gentle.

Blessed are those who hunger.

Blessed are the merciful.

Blessed are the pure in heart.

Blessed are the peacemakers.

Blessed are those who are persecuted for righteousness.

Those were the outcasts of the day, the ones who weren't the religious elite, the ones who were the outsiders.

It's no wonder then that we see the religious people getting annoyed and agitated each time he started to speak. It's no wonder that they react so forcefully and violently against him. It's no wonder that they plot and conspire against him and eventually put him to death.

It's no surprise because they didn't get what they wanted.

They didn't get the Messiah they wanted.

He didn't fit the bill.

So they're better off without him.

Have you ever felt you're not one of the gang?

Have you ever felt you're not in the crowd?

Have you ever felt you don't fit in?

Have you ever felt downtrodden?

Have you ever felt that you're being oppressed?

Have you ever felt everyone else gets while you don't?

Have you ever felt that you're the last on the list?

That anything bad that will happen will happen to you?

Have you ever felt you're not one of them?

You're not one of the religious elite?

Have you ever felt you could never attain to the rules?

Have you ever felt you don't even know the rules?

Have you ever felt poor in Spirit?

Have you ever mourned?

Have you ever sought justice?

Have you ever sought peace?

Have you ever felt like giving up?

Then God is on your side.

God came to this earth in the person of Jesus to show us His heart and how He wanted His people to live, in fact to truly show us all how to live. He has done this numerous times throughout the Old Testament to the people of Israel and He did it again through Jesus, only they didn't realise what was happening and they nailed him to a cross and killed him.

They didn't pay attention.

They didn't take heed.

They didn't listen.

They didn't realise.

They missed something beautiful and majestic that could've broken that cycle once and for all but they thought they knew better and so they nailed him to a tree.

For them, that was the better option.

They made a choice.

Not to listen.

Not to pay attention.

Not to take heed.

And they missed out.

The question that we are still left with is what will we choose? As the cycle seems likely to continue we are still left hanging with all those questions.

Loaded.

Pregnant.

Waiting.

Waiting for something to happen, when actually it already has.

In one of the most amazing turnarounds in all of history this was not the end because even when Jesus was on the cross and dying, he did not do what he was expected to do.

The Hairs Stand Up

CHAPTER SEVEN

Tom and John were walking home from school one day and saw a beautiful bike in the window of a shop. They both ran home to their mothers to ask if they could get the bike for Christmas. John asked his mother and she said that all he would have to do was to write a letter to Santa to ask for the bike. Tom asked his mother when he got home and got the same response, but having been in the school nativity play he thinks it might be better to write to Jesus, so he sat down and started to write:

'Dear Jesus, I have been a very good boy this year and deserve a bike.'

Rereading it he decided it may not be entirely true so he threw it away and wrote it again.

'Dear Jesus, I have been a pretty good boy this year, I think I deserve a bike.'

Again he thought this might not have been completely true so he threw it away and started again.

'Dear Jesus I haven't been that good this year but a bike might help me be good next year.'

Again he wasn't quite sure about the honesty of this approach so he decided to take a walk and start again later. While he was walking around the town he spied a statue of the Virgin Mary in the garden of one of the houses. Waiting until it got dark he sneaked into the garden and slipped the statue under his coat.

Once he got home he rushed into his room and started to write.

'Dear Jesus if you want to see your mother again, you better get me a bike.'

Like Tom, we can often think the whole story about Jesus shows him to be nothing more than some sort of genie-like man who can grant wishes and provide things for you. Often the way he has been portrayed has not helped and we can see why people like Tom would think that Jesus can get him something good at Christmas, I mean it was his birthday after all so he should know about getting some good presents! So we put him in our fairy tales and he fits in nicely with Santa, Rudolph, the tooth fairy and Shrek and so really it has no bearing other than being a nice little story.

A lot of people at the time did that too; they wanted this Messiah to set them free from their political oppression, to give them back their land and their rightful place as God's chosen people, but yet here they are watching him being nailed to a cross. For them this was the end of their fairy tale for this Messiah, he was obviously another phoney, another failure who didn't give them the ending they wanted.

And they weren't the only ones.

Even his disciples were left disappointed. They had spent the most time with him, they had walked, talked and slept in his company for nearly three whole years and they were still left with a sense of shock and awe when he died. Even though he had told them *exactly* what would happen, they were still shocked and amazed by what transpired as he hung upon a cross.

But there, in the midst of that scene, as he hung on that cross we hear a different story from a very unexpected source, a centurion, a man who had seen hundreds, if not thousands, of people die this way. As Jesus drew his final breath this centurion's words hang in the air saying 'truly this man was the Son of God'.[86]

These are very strange words for a mercenary.

For a man who saw thousands die.

This was just another day for him, another execution.

His break was coming up soon anyway.

But this isn't the only strange story we hear.

The next stories we find about Jesus are even more strange, even more fairy-tale-like.

A couple of days later, after he has been taken off the cross and buried in a tomb, a number of women are on their way to pour spices and anoint him. This in itself is not strange as it was a normal practice for burial in this region and in this time, but what they find when they arrive at the tomb is very strange indeed.

The stone that guards the tomb has been rolled away.

It is open.

The tomb is empty.

There is no one there.

It's quite freaky.

As I sit writing these words I am getting shivers.

I started to write about this tomb and Coldplay came on my computer as I wrote, one of their tracks called 'Fix You', and as it got toward the climatic ending I was writing that the tomb was empty and the hairs on my body began to stand up.

That's what it must've felt like for them as they discovered the tomb was empty.

He wasn't there.

Gone.

Now this meant one of a number of things.

Either his body had been stolen.

Or something else.

Something quite extraordinary.

Something unbelievable.

Something he wasn't expected to do.

These women ran home trembling, but ran with news.

The tomb was empty.

He was gone.

Risen.

Come back to life.

Resurrected.

This word and the words that they ran home to tell everyone changed the world; not just their world but *the* world.

What we find in the rest of the New Testament is exactly that, we have the words they ran home to tell everyone because they haven't stopped running. Ever since that day, ever since it all changed, people have been running to tell people the amazing news about it all, or as it's called in some places, the good news about Jesus.

All of the New Testament reflects that.

We find letters and stories from people who were there at the time, those people who followed Jesus around and watched what he did and heard what he had to say. These letters are to people, churches, friends and strangers telling them what has happened and how the world has changed forever.

Within these letters and stories, a new concept is introduced about a new covenant.

To the people who read and heard these stories, this new concept would have meant something, and to us it should mean something.

It means that the *berit,* the covenant that God made all those years ago with Abraham was being renewed; the relationship was being repaired and restored.

And it was being done through someone,

Whose name was Jesus.

He was the new covenant.

He was the something new.

These stories and letters record the words of Jesus who says himself that his blood forms the new covenant which is poured out for many for the forgiveness of sins.[87]

Blood?

Being poured out?

That's what happened to Jesus.

That's what happened as he hung upon the cross.

Before he was even nailed to the cross Jesus' blood poured onto the streets and left its mark.

It was left on the end of whips.

On bone.

On pavements.

On roads.

On hands.

And on feet.

It was left everywhere to be a reminder of what happened and what this new covenant cost.

When we saw the original covenant being made there was always a sacrifice that had to be made on man's part.

There was always something that had to be relinquished or given up to receive the blessing.

There was a cost and, like everything, when there is something to be relinquished, when there is a cost, there is obedience that is required.

For Noah there was the cost of doing something that everybody else thought was crazy.

For Abram there was the cost of leaving behind all he knew.

For Moses, he had to lead this frustrating bunch and even be punished for their grumblings and disobedience.

In each case there was a cost.

In each case there was sacrifice.

And to make a sacrifice requires obedience.

Each time God made a covenant with people, with His people, it required obedience but as we have seen this didn't ever happen and the cycle of obedience and disobedience continued.

Will this covenant make any difference?

I remember as I was growing up every so often I would hear people telling their stories about how they came to know about Jesus and how they are now followers of his. The ones that struck me the most were the really dramatic ones, you know the type; there's the ex-drug addict who met Jesus while he was out selling one night, or the murderer who met Jesus in her prison cell, or the kid who lived on the streets for a while but bumped into Jesus one evening in a back street.

There's a story of a man called Paul that probably shocked me the most, although I would also remember it as being the coolest!

Not because he had this badass wild-child lifestyle before, but because he went from being a follower of God who stoned and beat and murdered to being a follower of God who got stoned and beaten and eventually murdered; but it's better to hear the full story.

Paul was brought up as a Jew, the same religious group as Jesus and was a textbook religious child. He studied all there was to study and learnt from some of the most renowned teachers of his day. He loved his religion and his life and spent all his waking hours making sure he carried it out to the letter. He didn't like people who disagreed with his religion and when he heard about this man Jesus who was calling himself the Messiah he was overjoyed, until he found out that he didn't like what he had to say. In fact, you could go further than that because this man Jesus was being blasphemous and calling himself 'God' and that wasn't a good thing to do, so Paul followed and agreed with those people who nailed him to the cross. He also disliked all those people who were associated with this man Jesus and would go out with the mob to try and kill them as well, purely in the name of this religion and to make sure this blasphemous man's message was stamped out. He was there when the first of the followers was stoned to death[88] and carried on getting rid of them until one day when he was stopped in his tracks.[89]

He was on his way to try to get rid of some more of them when he was blinded and heard the voice of Jesus asking why he was doing all this.[90]

From that day on Paul's story became the story that he wanted to tell everyone about. His life was completely changed. He no longer pursued these people but became one of them, telling the story of this man Jesus and trying to correct people who were making the same mistake that he had been making all this time. He went on journeys to tell people about Jesus and ended up planting churches everywhere he went.

One of those places was a province called Galatia and Paul writes to the church he had planted there, where he had spent time and had nurtured and shared community and life.

He had already told them many things about Jesus and what he did.

They knew about the old and new covenant and how through the blood of Jesus the new covenant had restored and renewed all that had been before, but they needed to be reminded and so he tells them again that Jesus became a curse for us[91] because anyone who hangs on a tree is cursed.[92]

Jesus is cursed?

He takes this covenant and becomes cursed?

That's not the way this works.

Normally it's the other party who receives curse.

If God makes a covenant, as He did with Israel, they become cursed if they are not obedient.

But Jesus takes the curse?

He breaks the cycle?

Yes.

He does.

He was nailed to the cross.

His blood forms a new covenant.

He took the curse.

He broke the cycle.

He has enabled us to be in relationship with God in a new way.

But surely there has to be a catch?

Surely there is some cost?

Surely this requires obedience?

The old covenant required obedience so what would make this one any different?

Noah and Abram had to sacrifice so surely this new covenant will require obedience as well?

Obedience today is almost a dirty word. Nobody likes to be told to obey because nobody thinks they have to obey anything or anybody. Everybody has their rights and their say, everybody has their own way of doing things and everybody is encouraged to do their own thing. Immanuel Kant, who is considered by many to be the founding figure of modern philosophy, said some famous words which we have followed closely since they were formed on his lips:

'Dare to think for yourself.'

We dare.

We think.

We have our own thoughts and ideas.

We can do and think what we want.

Obedience isn't what we want to do.

Obedience is oppressive.

Obedience is the old way of doing things.

But really obedience is just hidden under layers of advertising and covered over with money and flashes so that we don't realise it but we are obeying the masters of consumerism or celebrity.

We follow David Beckham and obey his orders to buy a certain brand of underwear.

Or aftershave.

Or football boots.

Or sports subscription.

He markets a lot!

We follow the Apple symbol and obey its orders to buy the latest product.

We follow the advertisers and obey their orders to spray ourselves with a certain type of deodorant because then the women will literally run from every corner of the beach to be with us.

We all obey something.

We all follow somebody and do what they say.

Even if we don't realise it.

What we need to realise is that this is making us more enslaved than ever.

This is making us more similar to everyone else.

You don't have to walk far down the street where I live until you meet somebody who will be wearing the same or similar clothes as somebody you've passed minutes before. I have been to several weddings where the unthinkable faux pas has happened and two ladies have turned up wearing the same thing! I recently went to a concert in one of the largest venues in Northern Ireland which holds up to eight thousand people, and as we sat down my wife noticed that the girl in front of her was wearing the same jacket she had decided to take off minutes before we left home.

We are obedient but it is to the laws of fashion and so we spend our hard-earned money on the latest clothes.

We are obedient to advertisers and buy their product no matter whether we need it or not.

We are obedient to marketers and follow their trends.

We are obedient to culture.

So why can we not be obedient to Jesus?

Especially when it's free.

With no cost.

And no catch.

When he is the only sacrifice.

There is a story about Jesus as he was travelling around a number of cities teaching and preaching to anyone who would hear him. A lot of the people in these places weren't interested but some would come and listen to what he had to say. He saw a lot of people rushing about, working and trying to make ends meet. He knew that the message he had was the message they needed to hear but they just wouldn't listen. So as he walked through them he grew increasingly frustrated and prayed to God thanking him that his message was so simple that only the children understood. He then went on to say words that we need to hear today.

'Come to me all who are weary and burdened and I will give you rest, for my yoke is easy and my burden is light.'[93]

So how can you tell me there's no cost or catch?

He's talking about a yoke and a burden.

When Jesus talks here about his yoke and his burden he is not talking about the things that he was carrying. In this time and in this place these words were given to the teachings you would live your life by, given to you by one of your local Rabbis or Teachers. These people were the leaders of the day, they were the authority of the day and so you would follow the ways in which they taught you to live.

It was their yoke you lived by; it was their teachings that taught you how to live life well.

It was a way of life.

In the Old Testament the word 'yoke' was used most of the time when the oppressive regimes were talked about, when the Israelites were in slavery in Egypt or they were being ruled under authoritarian regimes.

There is no coincidence that this word is used by Jesus.

He tells the people, and he tells us now that his yoke is easy.

Today the advertisers, the marketers, the fashion powerhouses and the celebrities call us to obedience, and, whether we like it or not,

They tell us how to live.

That is a yoke.

Jesus calls us to something different because he says his yoke is easy.

It's no wonder the rabbis and rulers of the day didn't like his message, because it undermined their authority; it meant he was teaching something different and as people were flocking to him it meant that he was taking away their power and their control over the people. So time and time again the religious leaders try to trick Jesus by asking him questions that he will either not be able to answer, to try and make him less popular with these followers of his, or ultimately to force him to give them an answer that would break their laws and allow them to get rid of him; which of course we already know they did.

On one of these occasions they gather around Jesus and ask him a question:

'Which is the greatest commandment in the law?'[94]

In the book of Luke, which is one of the other accounts of Jesus' life it says that the man asked this question to try to trick Jesus.[95]

So Jesus answers the question and tells them that the greatest is: 'Love the Lord your God with all your heart, and with all your soul, and with all your mind. This is the first and the second is like it, you shall love your neighbour as yourself. Everything depends on these two commandments.'[96]

Jesus' way was a way of love.

Love of God.

And love of others.

Everything depends on these.

Everything you do and everything you say depends on these.

That was his yoke.

You didn't have to wear certain underwear, or smell a certain way, or wear a certain type of jeans, or go to certain stores; in fact it's not about anything that's on the outside at all.

His yoke was about love.

That was his burden.

Summed up in four lines.

Quite a difference from the 613 laws in the Old Testament.

Those are the laws the religious leaders were enforcing on the people.

The ways in which they had to act and dress.

Those are the laws they were asking Jesus to pick from.

And he came up with four lines.

Any advertiser would be happy with that.

Any marketer would snap up the person who could reduce 613 laws into four lines.

That's what Jesus did and that's what he showed.

That's what his yoke was all about.

How to love.

How to lead a life of love.

That's what he calls us to.

That is the obedience he requires of us, that we love.

Love.

And if we want to know how to live this life of love we only have to look to how he did it because obedience is seen in everything that he did and so we only have to follow and obey his life of love to be part of this new covenant.

To break the cycle.

To be in relationship with God in a new way.

When we do this we will suddenly find that our whole world will change and begin to be shaped into the world that was put into motion when it was discovered that the tomb was empty.

When that happened, a whole new way of life was opened up.

New possibilities were put into motion.

Suddenly the world doesn't have to remain as it always was.

There is hope.

There is opportunity.

There are new possibilities.

When we are obedient to Jesus and his yoke, his way of life, our whole world and the way we see the world will change.

That is why it is called the new covenant.

Everything will be made new.

And we can be a part of it all.

Final Thoughts

CHAPTER EIGHT

In this world that we live we want everything to happen in an instant.

We have fast food.

We have microwaves.

We have the internet.

We have phones that are getting smaller and smaller, yet still give us the chance to launch satellites into space with a well-designed app.

Our cars are getting quicker.

Our access to others is getting easier.

Our desire for speed is greater.

We want everything *now*.

Nobody wants anything tomorrow, we all want it now, or if it's possible we want it as soon as we think about it.

And so when you read those words on that last page I wonder if you wanted what it said?

A new hope.

New opportunities.

New possibilities.

And if you did, I wonder did your mind go back to the questions we asked earlier; those questions you would want to ask God; those things you may even want Him to stand accountable for!

If you did I wonder did you want them to be answered now?

This instant?

Because that's how we live.

We want it all now, we want that new hope, those opportunities and possibilities now, we want those questions answered now.

We want our world to change now.

The problem is, that doesn't happen often.

Seeing the world in a new way might take time.

Having your world change might take years.

That doesn't sit well with us, but our God is a patient God; there is no rush. As we see, through all the stories we've been told, there have been many times when people have had to wait, to sit in the midst of ashes having to scrape themselves with broken pottery to get some kind of relief.

That person would want change and would want it now.

But they had to sit.

To wait.

And often we do as well.

There are also stories that we've looked at where the main character didn't actually get to see the outcome in their lifetime.

They were given a promise but didn't see it fulfilled.

They were given hope but didn't see it spring forth.

I am one of those glass-half-full people, the ones who will see the silver lining, who will wait eagerly and enthusiastically for hope.

But I know the realities as well.

I know there are those who will not see that hope realised, who will not see the outcome in their lifetime.

I know and have listened as people have told me their stories of divorce and heartbreak, of the business friend who lost all the money, of the Christian boss who didn't really treat them very well. I have loved ones who have lost everything, who have lost their loved ones, who have been at rock bottom. I have sat with a friend of mine planning her funeral before she and her husband got to plan her thirtieth birthday party. I have friends who can hardly walk because of a degenerating disease and a friend who has had more operations than birthdays.

So I have seen the reality of despair.

Of loss.

Of hurt.

Of people who don't even want to hope anymore.

But I believe that God doesn't and won't ever give up.

I believe in a God of love.

Who, frustratingly, is also a God of patience.

And so we wait.

But as we do that, as we wait, keep watching as the world around you begins to change, as new hope appears, as new opportunities begin to arrive, as new possibilities unfold; as the way you see the world changes.

Because God will never give up.

May that be a call to obedience.

For us.

For our homes.

For our neighbourhoods.

For our towns and cities.

May it be a call to the nations to live a life of love and see the world change.

Notes

CHAPTER ONE: LET ME INTRODUCE EDDIE

[1] This particular love will only be known if you have seen *Anchorman*, and if you haven't it might make more sense when you get to Chapter Three.

[2] Genesis 1:26.

[3] Genesis 2:7.

[4] Genesis 1:26.

[5] Genesis 2:17.

[6] Genesis 2:23.

[7] Both these statistics have been taken from www.wateraid.org and their WHO/UNICEF joint monitoring programme (JMP) report 2012 update.

CHAPTER TWO: SORRY?

[8] Genesis 4:4–5.

[9] Genesis 4:8.

[10] Genesis 5:3.

[11] Genesis 5:6.

[12] Genesis 5:9.

[13] Genesis 5:29.

[14] Genesis 3:17.

[15] Genesis 4:12.

[16] Genesis 6:5.

[17] Genesis 6:6.

[18] Genesis 6:8.

[19] Genesis 6:9.

[20] Genesis 7:22.

[21] Genesis 1:28.

[22] Genesis 11:4.

CHAPTER THREE: WOODEN SHIPS AND SCALPELS

[23] Only three have had that privilege so far.
[24] Genesis 12:2–3.
[25] Genesis 12:1.
[26] Genesis 15:5.
[27] Genesis 9:11.
[28] Genesis 17:17.
[29] Genesis 22:12.
[30] Genesis 22:18.
[31] Genesis 3:24.
[32] Genesis 4:16.
[33] Genesis 25:7.
[34] Genesis 26:5.
[35] Genesis 25:23.

CHAPTER FOUR: REMEMBER HOW IT GOES?

[36] Genesis 15:12–16.
[37] Exodus 2:12.
[38] Genesis 15:18–21.
[39] Exodus 3:17.
[40] Exodus 12.
[41] Exodus 13:21.
[42] Exodus 14:16.
[43] Exodus 15:22–7.
[44] Exodus 16:4.
[45] Exodus 20:2.
[46] Exodus 32:1.
[47] Exodus 32:20.
[48] Numbers 14:20–3.
[49] Deuteronomy 28:1.
[50] Deuteronomy 28:15, 25.

CHAPTER FIVE: QUESTION MARKS AND POTTERY

[51] Ecclesiastes 1:9, amongst others.

[52] According to www.worldtoiletday.org, the toilet has added twenty years to human life expectancy over the past two centuries, and is crucial in preventing the spread of many disease, such as cholera. (Great for a tricky pub quiz question!)

[53] Genesis 4:5.

[54] Exodus 32:9.

[55] Exodus 32:10.

[56] Job 1:8.

[57] Job 1:14.

[58] Job 1:16.

[59] Job 1:17.

[60] Job 1:19.

[61] Job 1:21.

[62] Job 2:7–8.

[63] Job 42:3.

[64] Job 42:6.

[65] Job 42:7.

[66] 2 Samuel 7:16.

[67] 2 Samuel 7:23.

[68] Jeremiah 1:16.

[69] Ezekiel 2:3.

[70] Zechariah 1:3–4.

[71] Amos 5:6–8.

CHAPTER SIX: THE MAN WHO HAD EVERYTHING

[72] 1 Kings 3:10–12.

[73] This refrain is repeated many times throughout the book but first appears in Ecclesiastes 1:2.

[74] Ecclesiastes 1:14.

[75] Isaiah 1:4.

[76] Isaiah 2:12–22.

[77] Isaiah 54:10.

[78] Isaiah 55:3. All these references have been made through the book of Isaiah, however, they can be found as easily in any and in all of the other Major and Minor Prophets. These same themes of how far Israel has fallen, about what will happen if she remains in disobedience, about God's unmoved love for her, and of the hope of one who will come, run through all of these prophets words and so references could be used from any of the other prophets also.

[79] Malachi 4:2.

[80] N. T. Wright sets out a number of Messianic expectations that Israel would have had in the first century in his book *The New Testament and the People of God*.

[81] Matthew 1:16.

[82] Matthew, Mark, Luke and John are referred to as 'The Gospels' and depict the story of Jesus' life from four different angles. They were written or dictated from first-hand experience by his disciples or were written on stories told by his disciples and followers.

[83] Matthew 5:39.

[84] Matthew 5:44.

[85] Matthew 5:44.

CHAPTER SEVEN: THE HAIRS STAND UP

[86] Matthew 27:54.

[87] Matthew 26:28.

[88] Acts 7:58.

[89] Acts 9:3.

[90] Acts 9:4.

[91] Galatians 3:13.

[92] Deuteronomy 21:23.

[93] Matthew 11:28.

[94] Matthew 22:36.

[95] Luke 10:25.

[96] Matthew 22:37–40.